PLAYER NORTON

1

ROAD RACING

MICK GRANT

ROAD RACING

MICK GRANT

with Ian Beacham

Hamlyn
London · New York · Sydney · Toronto

Published by
The Hamlyn Publishing Group Limited
London · New York · Sydney · Toronto
Astronaut House, Feltham, Middlesex, England
Copyright © The Hamlyn Publishing Group Limited 1979
ISBN 0 600 36383 X
Filmset by Tradespools Limited, Frome, Somerset, England
Printed in Italy by New Interlitho, Milan

CONTENTS

Acknowledgements

The publishers are grateful to the following for the
illustrations in this book: Richard Adams; Allsport Photographic;
Vic Barnes; Ian Beacham; Budget Buy; M Carling; DPPI; Jim Greening;
W H Heaps; Brian Kelly; B Martin; *Motorcycle News*; Volker Rauch;
Sportography; Stream & Associates Ltd.

FOREWORD

The first time I came across Mick Grant was in the late 1960s when I had just taken up road racing seriously. He had started at about the same time as me, although he was a few years older.

I was watching a race at Cadwell Park and I noticed this big guy in black leathers with a bright red beard poking through the front of his Jet-Star helmet. I thought to myself: 'Who the devil is that old man', because I always tend to associate beards with people much older than me.

It didn't take long before the name of Mick Grant became familiar to me and one of our first tussles was at Croft in County Durham. He was a bit of a handful then!

I have raced against Mick perhaps more than any other rider and my opinion of the bloke has never changed: Mick is a superb rider, as his results over the years testify. On his day, he is almost unbeatable.

While he is a determined and very hard rider, he always adopts a mature, professional approach. If a race rests on the final corner and there is an almost impossible gap to make up on the leader, then Mick – like most of us sensible ones – would not risk life and limb trying to achieve it. He uses his head, rides well within his limits and I don't believe he would ever create a dangerous situation.

Being consistent at the top is not the easiest thing in racing and this is why I have always rated him higher than anyone in Britain. He also has so much experience to call upon, which helps him in every way on the track.

It would be unfair to label him just as a road circuit rider. He has shown that he can ride a bike of any category over every type of circuit and has what it takes to be a world champion. While I am perhaps not the man to talk about the TT, I have to say that his performances in the Isle of Man have been absolutely phenomenal. Away from the track, too, he has done a lot to improve the image of our sport, for which he is a fine ambassador.

He has always been known for his honest plain-speaking and this will be apparent throughout this book. Mick knows road racing inside out and there is no-one better qualified to describe the sport that gives so much pleasure to many thousands of people around the world.

Over the years, Mick and I have had some right ding-dongs in the big-bike classes and, while we might have leaned on each other at corners, there was nothing to complain about. In fact, we always have a good laugh about it afterwards.

I have always been especially keen to beat him at Scarborough, because he likes to perform well in front of his own Yorkshire crowd. One year we made an agreement to go hell for leather for the first 12 laps, cross the line together and then sort it out between ourselves in the remaining three laps. We both had a real go with our bikes touching at almost every corner. First I would dive up the inside, then he would do the same at the next bend. It was great sport . . . until his front wheel lost grip on some loose gravel and he went down. After I had collected the winner's laurels, we had a good chuckle about it in the paddock. That's Mick – a good sportsman and a marvellous road racer.

LIFESTYLE

Racing is what I want to do; nothing, but nothing, gives me greater pleasure or satisfaction than getting on that bike before the start of a race. I could never understand my father – he's been a coalminer all his life and still enjoys the job. I've been down the mines and just cannot see what he enjoys. But it is nice to know that people can be happy at what they do for a living. I think I'm very fortunate because I don't believe there are that many people who derive enjoyment from their livelihoods.

I know it sounds corny, but I count myself very lucky indeed to be a professional motorcycle racer. I am actually being paid to do a job which I consider to be the best in the world. I wouldn't want to do anything else. As a 20-year-old I was scared about not knowing what to do in the future; at the peak of my racing career the one major frightener was the thought that I would have to stop racing one day and come back down to earth.

It's a fantastic sport to be involved in. You might be going through a bad patch, like I had in 1978, and you think for a brief milli-second: 'Is it all worth it?'. Then you look around and realise it is. If you didn't have the downs in life you wouldn't know what the ups were. Stay level all the time, even by winning every race, and you'd soon be bored.

Mick Grant is known throughout the racing world as a superb craftsman. He earns his living by expertly piloting motorcycles at speed on all manner of circuits around the globe and his reputation as one of Britain's best has been built on years of experience.

Capable of beating everyone on his day, Grant has always been popular with race fans, young and old. Articulate, approachable, efficient, technically-minded, a master tactician and a winner – Grant thinks and talks intelligently about the sport with which he has had such a long and rewarding association.

Grand prix winner and the breaker of many lap records during his two-wheeled career, he has ridden a great variety of machines, from British four-strokes to Japanese two-stroke projectiles.

Along with Barry Sheene, Grant has been Britain's most consistently successful rider in the 1970s and he loves to comment on road racing as he sees it. As dedicated as he is passionate about his sport, the respect he commands from track rivals is immense and,

being the master of his art, Grant is looked upon as a model professional.

Of the requirements it takes to make a successful motorcycle racer, Grant considers natural ability to be very low on the list of priorities. Youngsters with natural ability are often seen at club level competition, but the majority of them fade into obscurity after a couple of eventful seasons.

I admire people with natural ability. Barry Sheene is the one who always springs to mind. His tremendous natural ability makes the job easier. People laugh when I say I have never possessed natural ability, but it's true. I feel I have had to work hard at what I'm doing, always having to graft at it to get somewhere. Yet at the end of the day, the job comes easier to me, because I know there are no short cuts.

The shining example of a man with more than his fair share of natural talent, says Grant, was Ken Redfern, whose brilliant track career ended when he died in a motorcycle accident on the public roads.

That man was just as happy going fishing on a Sunday as he was going racing, such a waste for someone with vast natural ability. Another one in the same mould is Gregg Hansford, but I don't think he's determined enough. Having

Rivals on the track, but friends off it: Mick Grant and Barry Sheene share a pre-race joke

opposite
Mick Grant – professional motorcycle road racer

13

this ability doesn't give you a divine right to success.

Hailwood was another – and he had the determination to go with it. But if Ken Redfern had possessed the determination and the enthusiasm for the sport that I have always had, perhaps he could have been a world champion. As it was, on his day, he was pretty well unbeatable.

Riders like Grant have shown that the lack of natural ability is no handicap if another quality is possessed: a sense of direction. He rates that as important if a rider is to have any chance of success.

When I began racing, I could have gone two ways. I could have gone into a lot of debt by taking out hire purchase on a G50 or a Manx Norton, emptying my pocket like a lot of other young lads did at the time and maybe being competitive, but spending six months of the year saving like mad because of an engine blow-up. The alternative was to use a ride-to-work machine and pay out just for petrol, entry fees and the odd clutch plate. This way I was getting in mileage and gaining so much experience. That was the direction I chose to start off with and it subsequently proved right.

Grant recalls fellow novices who did splash out on the proud Matchless G50 – a trusty, workmanlike machine – to try to achieve instant success. But many of them, in spite of enormous skill, are still contesting club meetings.

I had pals who started at the same time, but they were guys who liked their beer as much as their racing. They hadn't this sense of direction to make them understand which course to take. You have got to point yourself in the right direction all the time, whether it be deciding which factory to go to at the end of a year's contract or actually deciding which races you want to do and which you want to miss. Of course, it has to be said that the crystal ball comes into it – a lot is down to lucky long-term guessing.

Quite clearly, plotting out the right course does require a fair amount of intelligent thought and that's why most of the men who have made it to the top in recent years are informed, capable businessmen with a career of sound decisions and careful planning behind them.

Motorcycle racing today is a business for professionals and all the young go-ahead racers are little businesses in themselves. Those businesses, as with any business, will fail if they expand too quickly. Consolidation is all-important. You cannot go from club racing to world championships just like that. There has to be a firm footing to work from.

Grant feels that newcomers to the sport enter far too many classes and the bike sponsorship they get from a variety of backers is too great a millstone around their necks at

that stage of their careers. Enthusiasm to diversify into larger-capacity classes while trying to succeed on the smaller machines makes it much tougher for the lads wanting to do well. Grant feels the rush to get into the better publicised classes of racing instead of concentrating on gaining experience on 250cc and 350cc machines is detrimental to a career.

Although a motorcycle racing career is relatively short – it ranges from about eight to 12 years for most – it's still best to do a few years at the bottom end of the scale learning the ropes. But we're getting world champions emerging at 21. That's achieved by having 'big balls' and thinking that no-one is unbeatable. They stick out their necks, and get away with it for a year. At the other end of the scale, there's the bloke who has been at it for quite a while, who has a lot of experience and does not take chances and, by employing exactly the opposite approach, would still get the same results in a safer manner. That's the chap who has more chance of staying at the top.

Johnny Cecotto is the classic example. After winning his first title at 19, his career took something of a slump. He had the ability but he also had a very young head on his shoulders. The same happened to Sheene when he was hailed as the young superstar, but he managed to get over some rough times and went on to a great career with the help of what he learned in those early years.

Like Sheene and a number of other great riders, Grant mapped out his racing career at an early stage by making plans which he knew were within his capabilities.

You must know where you want to go. It's like going to the seaside: if you have a map, it's much easier to get there. You know precisely the way to go. If there is no map or signposts, you can take months to get there. You should know the direction in which you want to travel in life. That's common sense.

This sense of direction, which Grant feels is the all-important factor in any good rider's life, embraces all the qualities needed to succeed in such a demanding sport. The series of decisions needed to make a successful career can involve so many facets, such as the choice of bike to start on, which races to contest, the right mechanics to prepare the machine and much more.

You even have to consider whether you'll ever be able to make a living out of racing. Everything is in this sense of direction. Have this and, with enough work, you can get through. If you want to be a pianist and you can't play, it's no problem. You can learn – as long as you know that you want to play.

Grant turned his back on a possible teaching career and fought his way through an aimless period when he had a reputation as a 13-stone bearded beer-drinker with a penchant for the easy life, before finally realising

One way of keeping fit: Grant takes part in trials most Sundays during winter

that he could make something of life. He found his motivation in motorcycling.

But no matter how ruthless and hard-headed riders might be toward road racing, it will always offer a high entertainment value, as evidenced by the vast crowds which attend meetings with an international entry throughout Europe.

In this day and age, top racing is 60 per cent entertainment and 40 per cent sport. Entertainment at the highest level also has to be big business, of course, because of the large number of people putting money into it. While it should be kept as a sport, nice and clean and fresh, there is also an awful lot of money being invested. Those who bury their heads in the sand and say it should remain just a sport and shout 'long live the amateur' are being foolish. By the same token, it should still be sportsmanlike.

Road racing, according to Grant, is not a physical sport, apart from the TT and endurance racing. The accent is on mental pressure with the day's battle starting from the moment a rider signs on at 8.30 in the morning, while most spectators are still making their way to the track.

The fans can be a good ego trip or they can be very frustrating, especially if they come around when you're busy. It's important to keep your temper if a six-year-old who idolises you comes for your autograph when the engine is in

bits and there's 30 minutes to go. The same applies if a reporter treads on all the pieces lying about. I've perhaps lost my temper a couple of times and I felt bad about it afterwards. It's one of the frustrations of the job. When you've had a good meeting, it's no problem signing autographs until dark. As professionals, we should be consistent with the public whether we're winning or losing, but somewhere along the line you're going to upset someone. Ultimately it's the public who pay our wages so they should be given the utmost consideration. When they stop coming round, of course, it's time to start worrying.

Greater international media coverage helped to spread the star rider cult which, since the early 1970s, has made the personalities more important than the machines.

The top stars give good value to the manufacturers they represent. If they didn't they wouldn't be in that position. The public nowadays always want to see the stars, which is a change from the days when they went merely to see the MV Agusta or the Honda six.

Grant admits to getting a lot of pleasure from entertaining the masses, a factor worth far more to him than prize money; but he is fully aware that only results will satisfy the backers who provide his racing.

He firmly believes that crowds are being entertained more than ever before because of

The autograph hunters will always seek out their man, even if he's hobbling

circuits could do with proper grandstands and better toilets.

Grant once criticised Mallory Park in a newspaper column, labelling it the most dangerous circuit in the world because of non-existent run-off areas at the hairpin, which 750cc motorcycles approach at well over 120 mph. Circuit boss Chris Lowe jokingly queried whether he wanted an entry for the next big meeting there following this attack on the circuit.

Generally speaking, facilities for both spectator and rider are pathetic. In some countries, these so-called facilities are not only substandard, they are bloody degrading. But riders are in and out of this game so quickly that they've no chance to get things organised, unlike the officials who have perhaps had 40 years in the game and some, if not all of them, have hardly made any improvements to the sport.

In his last two years as a privateer before being offered a works Kawasaki contract in 1975, Grant was one of the few to make a useful living from the sport. But what riches! The best he could afford as transport was a three-litre, E-registered Ford Transit van and a five-year-old caravan. At the same time, he could spot runners who were obviously not making the sport pay, yet were running new Mercedes transporters, 14-foot caravans and more bikes and spares than Grant had ever ridden. When enjoying success as a talked-about privateer, Grant had three bikes running under his banner and considered himself most fortunate to be in that position. Now it's the rule rather than the exception to have that many at every level of competition.

Since 1974, a lot more money has come into the sport. At grands prix, it is most unusual to see anything as basic as a Transit van in the paddock, except at the very lowest level. This commercial injection of funds has changed everything. In 1974, the rust in the paddock would be on drivers' vans; now the only rust is on the perimeter fences. Commercialism and professionalism might frighten some, but it's for the good of the sport. The way for racing to succeed is for it to be more popular, which will happen through being commercialised. Commercialism at our level also spells out entertainment: it's now fun spotting all the different team colours on riders, bikes and transporters.

While the sport becomes healthier every year with the increased interest from outside concerns, Grant is terrified of the niggling rules and regulations that are often introduced by people who 'aren't switched on'.

The people who try to make rules on tyres have almost certainly never raced a motorcycle or, if they have, have never raced on 'slicks'. How can they make these decisions without the right advice? A lot of retrograde decisions are made with the right intentions but without taking the right advice.

the increasing commercialism of the sport and the immense amount of colour that this has brought to every meeting.

We're now well away from the black leather image, although racing in the 1950s and 1960s still provided good value for money, even if it did only appeal to the enthusiasts. Now it's far more a family entertainment – you can take the kids along.

His theory is backed up by the fact that the majority of spectators at motorcycle race meetings in the 1950s and 1960s came on bikes, whereas the emphasis swung the other way during the 1970s, with the bulk of the paying public being car owners and coming as families.

The sport would appear to have moved into a much healthier state. Enthusiasts will attend a meeting whatever the level of the entertainment, but you won't get families there unless it's good value. In the early 1970s, when the sport became more colourful and tidier with cleaner lines, the new professionalism caught the imagination of the public. There are now very few greasy machines in the paddocks.

He feels that the spectacle provided for the crowds rates highly, even though circuit facilities for paying customers may leave a lot to be desired.

The actual entertainment these days is as good as it's ever been, if not better, but some

In spite of changing status from a privateer to a fully-fledged works rider, Grant felt there was no gap to bridge and he was not conscious of moving into a more sophisticated world.

Only when I was with John Player did I become aware that I was in a different league of racing. They had a much stronger image-conscious approach to racing. You had to be there with a crease in your trousers that was sharp enough to cut. I found the whole contrasting scene slightly unreal. One minute I was with the team attempting to project an image, next I'd be scuttling off in a pair of overalls to get my own private bike ready. But as a works rider I try not to get involved with the preparation of the bikes. We each have our own jobs to do and, although I certainly don't mind getting my hands dirty, I've always considered myself a rider and not a mechanic.

Motorcycling fanatics fall into two categories – they're either mechanical people or they're racers. But at club level they're one and the same. Progressing in the sport, you meet those who get a kick from preparing the bikes and those who get their kicks from riding them. Anyone who's successful at racing will drop into the latter category.

Being used as a factory publicity vehicle, Grant realises that every time he goes out in a race he must do well – for himself and for his sponsors.

I know if I'm doing the job properly, to the best of my ability, that at the end of the financial year the money will be right. Of course, pressures are there as a factory rider. The guy on the other side of the fence knows if you're a works rider you have to be on the top of his list to win the race. Very often you know people are looking at you to succeed, but your first duty is to do the job properly. If I'm signed by a factory team, my personal standard is the standard they are buying and if that standard isn't high enough for them they shouldn't be buying me. I have never gone out in a race and not tried to achieve that personal standard. And I have never done a 'start money' special in my life. The first time I ever did that, I'd pack in the job. At the same time, racing isn't just about winning for me, although it is to some of those who pump in the money. For me it's a question of maintaining to my own personal satisfaction the standards that I have set.

As professional sports go, road racing is comparatively poorly paid, especially when the risk factor is taken into account. Golf and tennis have many big money-earners but full-time racers on really high incomes number no more than a dozen. As an established works rider, Grant will hope to make around £90,000 in a reasonable year – money which comes from his factory retainer, agreed start money from internationals, prize money and promotional fees.

If you go about it the right way, it's not beyond the realms of possibility to earn over £100,000 a year. People must appreciate that we are only at the peak of our trade for two or three years and I'm afraid the taxman hits us hard over that period. Our earnings are not spread over a lifetime. We still have to face many years when we have little chance of making a living.

Because professional racers have an opportunity to make decent money in a very short period of time before they end up on racing's scrapheap (unlike a doctor or a solicitor who can still practise at 65), it is unfair to criticise the large earnings which some of them make while at the top.

Many a racer in the past has finished up with nothing from the sport after entertaining tens of thousands of folks. I don't intend to be in that category, otherwise I'll have thrown away the best years of my life and, in my late 30s, I'll find I'm out of a job with no money. I'm sure no spectator would expect you to finish up that way.

The professional man starts with the bum jobs and when he wants to take it easier in life he's in a position to do that, but our role is completely reversed: we have the tit-bits first and the rough end of the stick later on, if we're not careful. But the public don't mind paying to be entertained, and the professional rider would like his portion of that revenue. He'd be a mug if he didn't. I just want to have my share for a rainy day. The law of the jungle exists in racing, just as it might in any office; the fit survive and the weak are pushed to the wayside.

For three years with Kawasaki, the team management agreed start money with track organisers and Grant's annual retainer embraced a sum that would cover negotiated fees.

He changed that in 1978 and immediately realised the sums he was negotiating were higher than those which Team Kawasaki had previously accepted.

We have to live with the start money system now, as opposed to having all the cash offered as prize-money and, as organisers are businessmen, they have to run their operation with profit in mind. They have to take into account how many people you are going to attract through the gates. So it makes it tough for the lower-graded riders; if they miss a meeting in protest against the offer made, the organiser isn't going to bother two hoots. Obviously, if an improved offer comes through after missing a couple of meetings, you haven't over-priced yourself.

A lot of riders race for far less than they should be getting and then complain afterwards. The trouble is that these blokes are enthusiasts who spend everything they have to go racing, even down to taking out second mortgages, and the most difficult thing for enthusiasts is to say 'no' to an organiser. The

Kenny Roberts on his
750cc four-cylinder
Yamaha

organisers realise this and take advantage of it.
I've always reckoned it costs nothing to watch
television on a Sunday afternoon and I would
rather do that than go to a meeting where I feel
I'm not being paid enough. The exceptions to
this are Grands Prix and championships where
I've a commitment to a factory.

But organisers, especially in Britain, are
much happier paying realistic start money to
riders with 500cc and 750cc machines than they
are to those with smaller capacity bikes. The
larger classes are the biggest draw for spectators because they offer the fastest racing and
the best riders.

As high fees are being paid to individual
riders to appear at a meeting – up to £5,000 on
most occasions – there is often the risk of the
'start money special', where a rider prefers to
settle for a safe placing, knowing that he has
already secured his money.

There are well-known riders who may do it
from time to time but they cannot do it regularly or they would soon be out of a job. Results
have to be achieved for them to be wanted by
other organisers. Even so, I could name riders
who compete purely for money. Maybe they
started off seeing it as a sport, but became spoilt
by the money. People do change and it must be
the most natural thing in the world for someone
who has had a good run at motorcycling to free-
wheel a bit if they plan to finish in a couple of

years. I'm not saying they should be doing it,
though. At the same time I wouldn't condone
them for doing it for financial reasons. All that
matters is that the end product is right for the
backers and that the rider provides a good day's
sport for a good day's pay.

Kenny Roberts, the brilliant American
who claimed a 500cc world championship at
his first attempt in 1978, was accused of short-
changing British fans at two end-of-season
internationals. Despite being paid something
in the region of £20,000 for the two meetings,
he brought only one machine.

I would never dream of going to a meeting
without two sets of leathers, oversuits, two
pairs of boots and two helmets so I'm prepared
for any eventuality. You should also have a
back-up bike to guarantee giving value for
money.

Roberts did only one race at each meeting
(Donington and Mallory) and disappointed
the vast crowds by winning neither. He was a
fool to himself. At the end of the day, it's him
more than anyone else who'll suffer – as will the
other professionals at a slightly lower level who
also do it. These lads can't be hungry for
winning.

Promoters are astute businessmen and can
accurately assess the amount of money
which will be taken at the turnstiles with
either Roberts or Sheene on the programme.

Most international riders with a crowd-pulling reputation can usually come to an amicable settlement with promoters although, throughout Europe, there are promoters who want even superstars to race for peanuts. Even in Britain, where road racing interest is healthier than anywhere in the world, certain organisers away from the powerful MCD tracks take advantage of the fact that riders have to contest every championship round and attempt to get them for as little as possible.

I have heard of one rider being paid £12,000 to take part in a British meeting and there have been rumours of similar sums being paid in Italy and France. But whether it's true or not, these would be very exceptional cases. Those kind of fees exist only rarely. I know I have never come anywhere near that sort of start money for one meeting.

But I must emphasise that money never has been and never will be a motivation for me to race, although careful thought has to be made to secure enough earnings to help when retirement inevitably comes. The position I am in is within reach of some riders who might be able to give me a tough fight on equal machinery, but who are still happy getting £50 a start.

The climb to the top of motorcycling's tree is a hard one and there's little chance of anyone making a quick fortune from it. If Grant divided the amount he has won in prize money by the amount he has spent getting to be a professional, the 'salary' for each year of racing would be comparatively modest. There are about a dozen British riders making a good living from the sport and a further 20 making a reasonable living. When Grant ran as a privateer, he made the sport pay its way as a business with sponsors supplying the bikes.

Although bikes, spares and transporters are getting far more expensive, there are also many more concerns putting money into racing. The average guy can't possibly afford to run a racing bike and find the necessary spares without outside assistance.

Racing success has brought Grant a six-bedroomed house set in 15 acres on hills overlooking part of industrial Yorkshire. He prefers Mercedes cars because they offer the comfort and reliability needed for his annual 40,000 miles of motoring. In keeping with the successful modern-day, professional sportsman, he has an accountant, a business adviser, a publicity agent (who searches out lucrative sponsorship and promotional deals) and a secretary for his well-organised fan club. A range of clothing and other goods bearing his name are sold at race tracks. As well as being keen on horseriding – he has two stabled at his home – and taking his off-road machines over his private scramble

Names on everyone's lips wherever motorcycles race: Australian Gregg Hansford (right) and American Kenny Roberts review the last meeting

course, he spends much of any spare time overseeing his own motorcycle accessories manufacturing company in Northampton.

Heavily involved in a variety of road safety schemes throughout the country and the holder of a motorcycle advanced driving licence, Grant appreciates that he has added responsibilities as a promoter of safe biking.

These campaigns make you consider safety a little more. When I took my advanced driving test, it wasn't an ego trip. I wanted to prove to people, especially youngsters, that I wasn't a lunatic and that I could take a pride in my driving. It gives them a yardstick: can they drive as well as me? Have they the right approach to riding as I have? It's a nice way, too, of putting something back into motorcycling. That's the motivation. Obviously, it helps your image, but most professional racers are happy to put in time and effort to try and reduce motorcycle crashes on the road; we're in a position where youngsters will listen to us and it would be criminal if we didn't put that time in.

Like many leading racers, Grant gauges his popularity after a season of competition by his position in the 'Rider of the Year' polls conducted by the weekly motorcycling press.

People only want to know winners. When you're at the top, everybody wants to talk to you; the moment you no longer command attention, these 'friends' disappear. When you're doing well there are many acquaintances you can approach to help start the sort of business that might keep you secure when racing comes to an end. But wait until you're over the hill and those openings disappear. I've seen so many riders finish their careers with nothing to fall back on. Looking at the number of people around the paddock who have never actually raced but who want to be involved in some way suggests there are plenty of opportunities to find assistance.

Being guest of honour at motorcycle club dinners, opening shops, sitting on road safety forums and serving on various road racing committees as well as interviews on local television and radio make winter rather more hectic than the actual racing season for someone like Grant. While he can see the promotional benefits of such activities, he finds them frustrating because there is nothing tangible to show for his efforts.

People might think we sit on our backsides once the season is over, but nothing could be further from the truth. As well as functions to take part in, there are all the following season's racing plans and finances to sort out. Personally, I enjoy the challenge of sorting out my bread and butter for the following year when it comes to negotiating contracts.

In spite of being one of the biggest names in such a glamorous sport, he leads a relatively quiet lifestyle, preferring the peace and quiet of his elegantly-furnished house to the

Grant the moto-crosser. He has also tried his hand at speedway

21

Grant sees even flat-out racing like this as a job: he often talks about putting on his 'overalls' when it's time to climb into his team leathers before the start of another race

never-ending string of hotel rooms that he uses through the racing season. For relaxation, his wife Carol and he occasionally dine out with friends, visit relations or shop for antiques. No late-night carousing for them!

His passion away from racing – and one method of keeping fit – is trials riding. Every Sunday in winter sees him tackling demanding sections on a genuine trials machine, often winning awards. To maintain a sensible weight, he also goes on cross country runs and sticks to a low carbohydrate diet. Apart

from a little wine when dining with guests, he rarely drinks.

Although often seen in jeans and tee shirts during summer, Grant is regarded as a snappy dresser, appearing in well-cut suits when required to attend functions.

Racers are blessed with a sense of humour. The sport they so keenly pursue and the effort required to do it calls for a human safety valve. Grant is known for his capacity to enjoy a practical joke or two and his career is spiced with amusing memories. A placid

temperament and an eagerness to relate a funny tale always win him followers.

He once sharply pulled up his tiny hire car in Finland to give two pretty female hitch-hikers a lift, but the smile quickly left his face when a squealing of rubber heralded the arrival into the rear of his vehicle of the car behind, driven by a German. Although the fault of the crash lay with the German, Grant and his partner – Dave Buck of Dunlop – agreed they would blame an Alsatian dog which they thought was about to run across the road. After some fierce arguing in conflicting languages, the police were called and the dispute resolved with diagrams.

The police showed us the drawings done by the German of what had happened and it showed, wrongly, skid marks from our car. I scribbled them out and put them behind his car. After a long period of silence, I asked the officer what was going to happen. A smile broke across his face as he said, speaking in English for the first time: 'I think we punish the German!'

Carol helps Grant to carefully put his tear-off visors into place

PREPARATION

opposite
Grant on the 750 Kawasaki at Donington, typical of the modern breed of race tracks

It is to the grands prix that the ambitious rider must look to measure his ability against the best; while he might know every bump and ridge on circuits in his own country, unfamiliar tracks present fresh challenges.

As well as racing on British circuits for almost half the year, Grant tests at least twice a month on the same tracks and so has built up a detailed knowledge of them.

While he knows through experience precisely how to set up his machines for any one home circuit, however, a visit to a European track that will be seen only once a year requires a great deal more time and effort.

The many hours spent travelling between grands prix, some of which fall on successive weekends, reduces the amount of time available to the rider and his mechanic to successfully prepare the bikes.

Domestic race meetings are almost all within a few hours' motoring from Grant's Yorkshire home, although he makes a point of staying in a comfortable hotel near the circuit the night before an international – this eliminates any risk of being late for the start of practice. Before he began to earn a living from the sport, he would sleep in a small tent or in the back of his van.

Even now, many riders in the paddock can be seen wheeling their bikes out of the van at night and replacing them with sleeping bags. It's a question of economics for the privateer, although I don't think it really matters where you sleep. The night before a race, especially if you're keen, you hardly sleep anyway. But it's possibly more important for a privateer to be by the circuit the night before because his transport can frequently be unreliable.

Whereas home meetings often have one day of practice split into ten-minute sessions, a custom which Britons accept without question, grands prix allow two and a half hours practice for each class, spread over two or sometimes three days.

By competing only at British meetings, a rider can stay at home, service the bikes and confidently plan for the next races. But the world championship rounds present a different picture: away from home for long periods, often with little time for either works runners or privateers to get their machines fettled before the next meeting, adequate stocks of tyres, chains, brake pads and other components have to be carried.

When spares are in short supply, the members of the travelling grand prix 'circus' will attempt to beg or borrow the necessary components from fellow competitors, long since an accepted practice of the sport.

With the right pre-planning it's advisable to be self-contained but, such is the spirit among the grand prix riders that most will help out one another. Sometimes you can be too well organised. When I carried a hydraulic big end press around with me, it was difficult to turn away those who regularly wanted to borrow it, even though it would often be returned worse for wear.

First there gets pole position in the paddock: nearest to the taps and the electricity and furthest away from the smelly toilets. But you have to establish a working area and I'm sure there would be less hassle if paddocks were bigger. At somewhere like Francorchamps in Belgium, which has a minute paddock, if one arrives late even with the right passes, there's one devil of a job to find anywhere to park. The situation isn't much better in many British paddocks, which can be full of cars that have almost no right to be there.

But I still feel strongly in favour of the public being allowed access to the paddock, where they can talk to and actually touch the stars. Once we lose the personal contact between rider and spectator, as some legislators are trying to do at GPs by having the public barred, the crowds might lose interest. We do not want a Formula One car situation to exist in motorcycle racing.

Restriction of public access at some Continental meetings was instigated after reports of theft from riders' property but, although there have been instances of pilfering at British events, Grant has only lost a wristwatch (at Donington Park) and a crash helmet (put down for a second on the pit counter at Imola). He accepts that some items of raceware might be eagerly sought after in such countries as those behind the Iron Curtain, where an unattended transporter can lose all its stickers in a moment.

We only draw the line at roping-off a section for the bikes to be prepared efficiently, so that tools and parts won't be trodden on and mechanics won't be bothered when they have to do an important job. As I see it, the contact is with the rider, who is generally accessible to the people at all times other than when he is actually out on the bike.

following page
Grant on the Kawasaki 250cc in-line twin on which he won his first European grand prix in Holland

The battle for world championship points commences months before the grands prix are staged. Riders not known to certain grand prix organisers and even those who have made names for themselves in their own countries, can spend weeks waiting for official confirmation that their entries have been accepted. Many GP officials do not even bother to reply to riders desperate to know if a long haul to a foreign circuit will end in a curt refusal of a start. For many, this can be the biggest stumbling block to any future grand prix career.

It's a ridiculous situation when some of the best riders in the world find themselves arguing with the organisers because they have been refused a start – it happened to Kenny Roberts. If the champion has problems, what does the up-and-coming youngster have to face? You can send as many letters as you want to some GP organisers and they just won't correspond. It's a joke. Some places involve travelling a long way even if you are guaranteed a ride; it seems ten times further if you're turned away. But the only way to become established is to fall into line with the ways of these organisers: it's totally wrong and totally unprofessional, but nothing has been done to change the system.

The FIM minimum guarantee fee for GP contestants without a record to back up a claim for more money stood around the £100 mark towards the end of the 1970s – which would certainly not even cover travelling expenses for many. As a recognised rider and following a successful GP season, Grant could still command only £140 from each grand prix yet his hotel bill might amount to double that. Even when Barry Sheene was the biggest draw of all, his payment for each world championship round was a paltry £400.

It is an ironical fact that the grands prix attract the biggest crowds of any races we compete in, yet they pay the poorest. Some of the attendances are remarkable but the clever organisers know that you have to go to their round if you are serious about the championship. Every round should have its financial books closely examined and, ideally, after allowing the circuit a reasonable profit, all other income should go back to the riders, either in start money or in prizes.

On the other side of the coin are rounds like Jarama in Spain where most of the spectators seem to be policemen and, because they must be losing a few thousand pounds, it seems clear to me that such a meeting doesn't warrant grand prix status. Although I always campaign against anything being closed down, the championships should be run on business-like lines; if they aren't financially viable, the riders shouldn't have to go for nothing just to chase vital points.

The purse at each grand prix should be based on a percentage of the size of the crowd.

If somewhere like Jarama did not have championship status and riders could negotiate realistic start money, the Spanish organisers would not even bother to ask the FIM for a date on the racing calendar. They know it would be a colossal financial disaster.

When Grant began to race in grands prix, his fixed plan was to do only those rounds at which he would be accepted and which would give him the feel of the classics.

By taking in other international meetings he was just able to cover his grand prix costs. As a contracted Kawasaki runner five years later, the decline in the buying power of the FIM start money meant that he finished his GP season showing a loss!

The grands prix in 1978 cost me money – and I was one of the lucky ones because I had no mechanics to pay (they were Kawasaki UK employees) and no bikes to find. I had only to get myself to the meetings which, with a fairly heavy UK racing commitment, meant considerable air travel.

The grands prix are now so competitive that to finish in the top ten in any class is a remarkable achievement. Every rider is fully aware that only race winners attract the all-important press coverage which can open up a whole world of sponsors. Sponsorship is often the greatest hurdle to surmount. Those prepared to offer enough cash to support a season's racing are few and far between.

Many youngsters today think sponsors just drop out of the sky and those who do land a good backer often fail to give their benefactor a decent return, not in terms of money but more in the way of repaying the favour the rider is being given. I have met young riders who think they're God's gift to racing. The way some talk so matter of fact about getting rid of one sponsor and taking on another makes me sick.

To be a worthwhile proposition to a sponsor, the rider has to be a saleable item. At the highest level, this means having looks which are promotable enough to go on a poster and having the personality to handle any publicity schemes. Any big sponsor has to off-set his expenditure against what he can expect in column inches in the press or in TV time. But for every top rider who can attract multi-thousand-pound deals, there are a hundred others who feel lucky to have someone merely provide a couple of machines for the season.

Some might see motorcycling sponsorship as somewhat 'Mickey Mouse' compared to the Formula One car world, but our sport can attract firms with the sort of money which would not get them anywhere in the car racing scene. It is my belief that car sponsors will one day realise what a family entertainment motorcycle racing is and they will put their money into a sport from which they really can benefit. I may not be the best rider in the world

but I am very happy with the number of occasions I have appeared on television in a year.

As well as sponsors who are content to plough a lot of money into racing through their enthusiasm for their sport, many motorcycle dealers have discovered the benefits of rider support.

I know many of them wouldn't go near the sport if there was no return for them. They look upon road racing as a business and from my associations with dealers in the past I know that column inches can be translated into bike sales.

The power of the press must not be underestimated. In England, we have publications that are read throughout the world so that if a guy cleans up in this country he is going to be read about all over the place. That's how you establish a name in Europe. Dudley Cramond captured a lot of headlines through his riding style and, perhaps for the wrong reasons, he has become known.

The John Player Norton team knew the value of publicity with Dave Croxford. They had a bike which proved to be inconsistent, so the only way they could attract some press coverage was to have Croxford clown about. Unfortunately, just getting good consistent results is not enough. A rider has to be a good vehicle for publicity as well: column inches do count.

The closer you get to the pressmen, the more coverage you can get, if you're worth it. Fostering good press relations is important, if only because journalists are people we have to work alongside and I'd sooner be working with friends than not. If I was working for a team whose manager I didn't like, the worst thing in the world would be for me to fall out with him, because we all have to work together. Living away from home for much of the time, the more friends you can have around, the more enjoyment there is.

The advice Grant offers anyone contemplating a racing career, no matter what their nationality, is to race for several years in Britain, where the sport is healthy and is covered by a specialist press that is read worldwide. Once a rider is established, a good sponsor will almost certainly be found and the way to go then is to select internationals in Europe to promote the name. South African Kork Ballington, who won two world championships in his first year of signing a full works contract with Kawasaki, mapped out his career on those exact lines – and succeeded.

There are still those who insist they must go straight into grands prix and every year they face a financial battle. Every winter, they struggle to gather up enough money and their resistance has got to weaken.

Once a youngster earns a place on the grading list of his country's organising body (which allows him to go grand prix racing)

and is fortunate enough to be accepted by the organisers, there is still no guarantee he will be in the race. Such is the competitiveness of world championship racing in each category that a mere second in time might cover up to a dozen of the fastest riders in practice. No wonder the experienced GP runners claim that qualifying is harder than the actual race!

Two miles of almost perfect riding in practice can be ruined by one missed gear or by being baulked by someone. You find that your lap speed is just not quick enough and so off you have to go again.

Apart from a trip to Tilburg in Holland, Grant's first venture outside Britain was as a member of the John Player Norton team. Booked to travel with the team from Harwich to the Swedish 750 championship round, he missed his connecting train at Liverpool Street station in London, but felt he had a chance of catching the boat after cajoling an old Volkswagen Beetle from a Hertz rental receptionist. His reckless drive to the Essex port now leaves him shuddering, although at the time he considered it would have been disastrous to miss the sailing.

If I was now in that situation I would get on a 'plane from Heathrow. But I lacked the experience at the time, and my only thought was to catch that ship. The car trip was a nightmare: I just missed a JCB excavator backing out of a road; as I had built up my speed to 70 mph or so, I was going to get through the ever-closing gap come what may. Then, with ten minutes left, I could see the dockyard – and I went the wrong way up a one-way street full of roadworks, bouncing over planks, compressor hoses and tools. Workmen were bobbing out of holes to see what the din was all about. I dumped the car on the quayside and leapt aboard just as the gangplank was being removed. There was an old chap sitting on the quay, dressed in wellingtons and a blue rolled-neck jumper. I gave him the car keys, a quid for himself and shouted 'Hertz' at him. As the ship moved out I don't think he had a clue what I was saying. I was on board for three hours before I got my breath back.

While some riders still prefer to spend time with a rotary file working on their engines, the successful ones are doing their circuit homework before the start of a major meeting.

I have been appalled to hear factory riders ask which way the circuit goes when they prepare for first practice – they have not been joking, either! But we are in an age where people can do half a dozen laps of a circuit unknown to them and then break the lap record. I find that incredible. I am incapable of doing that – I need as much pre-event preparation as possible and by adopting that approach I like to think that I can go through each racing season successfully as a professional and still finish in one piece.

31

When the bikes are wheeled out of the transporter and notes from the previous season are studied, the first task for a rider and his crew is to determine the correct gear ratios for the circuit in question. By achieving a fast practice lap as early as possible – a priority for everyone in case the weather deteriorates – the right size cogs for the gear-box and the rear wheel have to be found quickly.

It's often wise to forget about setting-up the bike perfectly at the beginning of practice. Putting in a good lap in the first session can pay off if it begins to rain during the other two practice periods. That happened at Assen in 1978 when my first session time was good enough to give me pole position because it rained during the other sessions and caught out a lot of others. Works runners can be seen messing about with their engines during the first session and they discover they've an awful job on their hands even to qualify when the weather turns to rain.

Correct gear ratios are usually found by ascertaining the likely speed on the fastest straight and remembering what was used on a similar straight at another circuit. It's a trial and error task for some although many will only be a tooth away from having the right size cogs.

If you're going down to something like a 13-tooth cog on the front sprocket, horsepower will be lost through movement of the angles of the chain. The faster the circuit the bigger the front sprocket, which absorbs less power and reduces chain wear. All gear ratios are normally worked out from the gearbox output shaft, which remains constant.

Considerable time is spent consulting gear ratio charts to get the best marriage of front and rear wheel sprockets and some riders will deliberately use high gearing for slow first and second gear corners, sacrificing speed on the fast straights to gain an advantage over their rivals. But at an ultra-fast circuit, such as Spa Francorchamps in Belgium (where bikes can average over 130 mph) gearing has to be for top speed.

Although every circuit requires different gearing, the beginner's rule of thumb is to get maximum revs just before knocking off the power at the end of the fastest point of the circuit. But even that's not quite true – there's no set pattern, it's all down to where you are going to get maximum advantage and basing the gearing on that section. In some races where you have a fairly slow machine, you have to gear it higher than it can theoretically pull in the hope of getting a tow from a faster bike.

From an engineering point of view and for the good of the transmission, Grant sees the ideal sprockets as a 14 or 15 on the gearbox and a 30 to 35 tooth rear sprocket, although these ratios vary considerably from one machine to another. Less than a 14 on the

Grant and his mechanic can still smile, even though the bike refuses to run. His first full-time mechanic in the early 1970s was paid £10 a week: 'If people want to do something badly enough, money won't be the important thing,' says Grant.

On ultra-high speed tracks where bikes are travelling at up to 180 mph for long distances, a slick tyre is sometimes unable to stand the pace, and the cover deteriorates in this way

gearbox will lead to excessive chain wear, especially on a fast circuit. Four minutes is all that it should take a competent mechanic to change sprockets.

Mechanics, however, come in all shapes and sizes: Grant divides them into three groups. The first group are those who think they know all about tuning, but whose lack of ability invariably leads to mistakes.

Some start to learn the trade in a garage, have a couple of years with a privateer and, when they finish up in a works team, they suddenly become grand prix mechanics, miniature gods. But the only obvious qualification for a top mechanic would seem to be experience.

The second category, into which Grant put his long-serving spannerman Nigel, is that of good, honest workers who don't try diving into engines or altering compression ratios but who can change components as efficiently as the best in the game. They can be trusted to do just what is asked, which gives the rider confidence in his machine.

I'd much rather have one chap from the second category than a dozen from the first. Mechanics at grand prix level aren't idiots, that's for sure, but the wizards who can actually make a bike go quicker are few and far between.

The third and best group are, in Grant's words, 'akin to rocking horse droppings' –

extremely rare. These are the clever mechanics and number no more than a handful in the whole racing world. Kel Carruthers, an ex-world champion and the mastermind behind the magnificently-prepared Yamahas of Kenny Roberts (the American who won a world title at his first attempt) is the name Grant puts at the top of the list through his sheer technical brilliance.

Ken Suzuki, now manager of the Kawasaki UK technical team, once suggested to an astounded Grant that good riders were easy to find but mechanics were not.

It eventually occurred to me he was right. A rider can be checked by the watch and seen to be doing well, but there is little you can do to immediately check the qualities of a mechanic.

Being a race mechanic calls for an inexhaustible supply of enthusiasm and, sometimes working for days on end with next to no sleep, a capacity for work that few jobs can demand; Grant was once annoyed to hear Kawasaki mechanics asking for overtime payments on top of their normal standard rates – a request unheard of in racing!

The dedication needed to be a mechanic at top level is so enormous that time shouldn't enter into it. If teams had to pay double time to their mechanics, many would not be able to afford to go racing. Those mechanics employed by factory teams often enjoy the best of conditions: they eat well and sleep in hotels. But there are dozens of others who have to spend the night in the back of a van. It all boils down to what you want to do in life. Quite obviously, these lads want to act as mechanics and don't mind what they have to endure.

Before he took on his first paid mechanic, Grant would attend to his own engines while his wife, Carol, cleaned the bikes. Even though he had a full-time job he was keen enough to work on the bikes until the small hours of the morning, throughout the week.

It wasn't work. It was fun. Racing has never been work for me.

For many riders, however, tyres are the biggest headache of all. Tyres for racing motorcycles now come in all shapes and sizes and the man who has a contract with one of the big manufacturers has a massive advantage over those without any tyre company support.

There are several different compounds for different circuit surfaces. Those that are non-abrasive, like the smooth purpose-built Brands Hatch or the public roads of Imatra (scene of the Finnish Grand Prix) which become shiny with a coating of rubber and oil from everyday traffic, call for a tyre with a soft compound, but a much harder product is needed for rougher track surfaces such as Assen or Donington Park.

The critical factor is the tyre's optimum working temperature when, within a range of

a few degrees, it will give its best in terms of grip. For high speed circuits, tyre pressures are increased to reduce movement of the carcass and so cut down the risk of the tyre overheating.

It would be difficult to get a hard compound tyre to reach its working temperature on a slippery surface, so a soft tyre would be called for and vice versa on a rough-surfaced track. Put a soft tyre on a super-abrasive surface like Assen, and you'd be on your ear after three laps.

Acting on the feed-back of information from leading riders over the years, tyre companies have produced intensively researched tyres to meet the demands of the modern motorcycle. Technicians of the major concerns who service the top teams at internationals all over the world have the knowledge to advise riders what to use. Grant is one of many who will be involved in long discussions with them to ensure he has the right tyres for the job.

Of course, there is more to it than choosing a compound. There's the tread pattern to consider when it's wet and the choice of profiles. Mix that with the combination of track surface, the speed of the circuit, the bike and the weather and there are about a thousand variables to ponder – and the right combination is going to win you the race in most cases. It's like bingo.

On a dry day, when most riders have slick tyres back and front, these might all look the same to the layman, but those who make a good start and fall back after a few laps can often blame the wrong choice of tyre compound rather than any deterioration in rider or machine performance.

A slick tyre in dry conditions cannot be bettered and will sometimes be superior to a patterned tyre in the wet at a place like Donington, which has a porous track surface cleverly designed to take away excess water.

The full 'wet' tyre is used when it is actually raining, leaving water actually lying on the track surface and the detailed pattern of the tread is designed to try and combat the aquaplaning effect.

When the track is only partly damp and is basically almost dry, intermediate tyres are used. The idea behind these slightly patterned slicks is not to clear water; they are cut in such a way as to allow gentle flexing of the tyre surface which encourages a rise in temperature. Consequently, as such a tyre becomes hotter in a much shorter time than an ordinary slick, it is soon performing at its best – essential to counter the uncertain damp patches of the track.

Normal 'bald' slick tyres will not perform in the wet because conditions prevent them from reaching their ideal working temperature, although Grant insists that such a tyre

While Pat Hennen soldiers on, Grant appears to be testing his tyres to the limit!

from one type to another): two laps may be needed on a cold afternoon to warm up slicks while only three-quarters of a lap may be all that is required for a patterned cover.

Complications occur with the fitting of different tyres to back and front wheels: while the rear tyre – the one that takes the greatest pounding – can be at the ideal temperature after a single warm-up lap, a similar cover on the front, which is only put under stress during heavy straight-line braking, might be nowhere near hot enough to grip the surface effectively.

A mixture of rear slick and front patterned tyres would probably both take the same time to hit the required temperature. Many riders have the ability to correct a rear slide, but losing the front wheel usually spells disaster, so it is imperative that the leading tyre choice, as well as being compatible with the cover on the back, also offers the most grip of the two.

The tyre situation is as complicated as the particular rider wants to make it. I have gambled in the past by using a type of tyre against the wishes of the company who have provided that tyre and I've still come out on top. At other times, the gamble has failed. Then there have been the occasions where I have come off the bike because the wrong compound was fitted. It is a problem, but one that is here to stay and there would be far more accidents if the wooden-heads had their way in insisting on an FIM rule to make riders use one universal tyre. A universal tyre would be unable to cope with the power and the 130 horsepower machines would be replaced by 60 horsepower bikes. What good would that be to the progress of the sport?

will still provide grip once it is warm, even on damp patches.

The whole idea of a slick is to get more rubber onto the road. As it has no grooves, there's a bigger area in contact with the road and, if that patch of rubber can generate enough heat to become grippy, even on damp areas, then that will work better than a treaded tyre.

Proof of the capabilities of slick tyres came at Assen, when the 750cc machines continued to circulate just short of lap record time in light drizzle. By that stage of the race the tyres had been used enough in the dry to be at their most effective and even the damp surface failed to significantly reduce their grip.

But riders who start on intermediate tyres can be caught out if a track dries out completely during a race. The tyre's instability will lead to overheating because it is not designed to run in completely dry conditions. Handling will then become difficult.

The racing tyre, of course, is no longer made entirely of rubber and at high temperatures the synthetic materials from which it is constructed often emit some oil, which can lead to wicked slides.

What surprises Grant is the common belief that only slick tyres require a warm-up lap. All modern tyres have to be brought up to their required temperature (which varies

Following the warm-up lap, Grant will touch his tyres to check temperature and, if he is still uncertain about whether they are warm enough, he will have no qualms about taking it easy for the first couple of laps.

Some dim organisers have a lead car ahead of the bikes on a warm-up lap. But as that's only going about 60 mph round the bends, it gives our tyres no chance to warm up. To overcome that, you must either pass the car and risk exclusion or wait on the line until the vehicle is well out of the way and then blast round. At the Macau Grand Prix, we once had to follow a single-cylinder Yamaha roadster. It just goes to show how much the rule makers know about tyre development. They still believe you only need sharp edges for grip, which is rubbish. The more fresh air allowed on the tyre surface on a dry day, the less effective the grip is, but try telling that to some of the technical committees. Those making the noise are guys who rode Manx Nortons which were only fitted with a universal tyre because they knew of nothing better to race with at the time.

Grant defends tyre companies like Dunlop

and Michelin from recent criticism that they now play the decisive part in racing.

Any ruling that eliminates slicks will be harmful because we just cannot do without the variety of compounds needed to cope with the sheer power of the modern racing bike. And it has to be said that when people call some races processional because rain catches out the bikes shod with slicks, there can be some interesting developments going on downfield involving riders who have made clever decisions over their choice of tyres.

When slicks were first paraded in front of are amazed public, some related them to bald car tyres which, without any tread, had difficulty obtaining any grip on the road, but a smooth tyre on a car is one past its best; a slick was designed to run on four millimetres of compound.

Having ridden on slicks since they were first introduced, Grant feels they are streets ahead of the old patterned tyres, of which a popular example for fast circuits was the Daytona-type, flat-bottomed Dunlop KR97. But at speeds of 140 mph in a straight line, the bike would begin to weave and unless the power was rolled off, a tank-slapper would develop. Stiffening of the tyre carcass did, however, cure the problem.

Tyre development by the big companies always falls on the side of safety – just. But if they don't go to somewhere near the limit there's no way of knowing how much further they can progress. Although tyre design has come on in leaps and bounds, I am still staggered at the number of combinations that can be done with a black, round piece of rubber to make it perform in so many different ways and so differently from week to week. Yet I believe tyre design is still in its infancy.

During the first part of a grand prix practice session, perhaps while gently bedding in new components, a rider like Grant will use the important laps to 'scrub' in a new set of tyres; these are then taken off the bike and remain untouched until race day.

The correct jetting for the carburation can be critical, more so with a disc valve induction two-stroke than with a piston-controlled machine, and especially with mid-range jetting. Varying temperatures, altitudes and the humidity levels of circuits are just some of the factors that will determine jet sizes.

If a rider is fanatical about jetting – and I'm not – the ideal place to base the setting is where the engine will run weakest, which might be at the lowest part of the circuit, the most heavily-wooded or on the longest straight.

The heat range of the sparking plug might also be changed during those vital two and a half hours of practice for a grand prix. On a fast circuit, the 250cc and 350cc Kawasaki racers needed a very hard plug; although this had an effect on starting, a softer grade might

have resulted in a holed piston or detonation.

Being a very individual sport, some riders might strip their bikes down between the end of practice and the start of a grand prix. Any doubt about a two-stroke motor will see the head whipped off for a cautionary check inside.

Towards the end of practice I do like to 'chop' the engine, wheel it back to the paddock and, although a reading is usually a good guide towards checking if the carburation is correct, I pull the head off to have a close inspection of the pistons. Because the quality of petrol varies so much from country to country, there's always the risk of detonation. This nibbles away at the piston and may not show on a plug reading. For a 20-minute practice it might give no trouble but in a 90-mile race it almost certainly would, perhaps resulting in a seizure or loss of power. Whipping off the head after practice is a modern two-stroke disease, but we're learning new dodges all the time to cure things like detonation, including such things as slightly bigger tail pipes to reduce back pressure.

But really, if you're spending too much time getting the thing perfectly set up, it's time that would be better spent learning the circuit. Steve Baker spent 1977 comparing Dunlop with Goodyear and Michelin at almost every circuit and his racing suffered. He would have been better sticking to one brand of tyre even if it wasn't the best. There's so much, in theory, to do to get the bike properly set up that several of the different stages I've mentioned would not be touched, even if you have highly experienced mechanics, because, at the end of the day, it's a quick lap time that counts.

There are so many pre-race variables that the whole thing can never get boring and every weekend offers a completely fresh challenge. To the outsider, the picture might appear the same from one month to the next but, on top of all the mechanical activities, there are outside pressures for the rider to consider, such as distractions from press stories on your poor form in a bad season, or speculation on whether you can maintain your success rate in a good one!

While a number of riders wear polystyrene back protectors (as used by horse jockeys) to reduce skin loss in the event of an accident, Grant now prefers to ride without one. Neither does he have pads zipped into the knee sections of his leathers, because his tucked-in style presents no danger to his body when cornering. Until experiments in the United States produce a better man-made substitute which offers more protection, won't burn the skin upon impact with the track or be as supple, leather will continue to be the only material suitable for racers.

Grant's racing suits are made tight, but gradual give in the leather allows the suit to perfectly mould to the shape of his body.

The polystyrene foam back-protector is favoured by some riders for the faster circuits, where there is a risk of substantial skin loss in the event of an accident

body which can take a pounding in a crash are often double skinned, with the team name sewn over the original layer of leather to add thicker padding on the arms and legs. Leathers are carefully designed to offer the rider good protection, even to the extent of having the rider's racing number in leather on the back, another part from which there can be a terrific skin loss in a tumble.

It's frightening to see some of the lightweight leathers in use today. Poser's leathers really. Mine are always made from heavy leather but those worn by the tiddler bike riders to save weight seem to be made of tissue paper. When they fall off, they'll lose a lot of skin. Because your life has surely got to be the most important consideration, good quality leathers for all riders are vital.

With an obligation to a factory to look smart, Grant prefers to display new leathers instead of patching holes caused by tumbles or knee scrapes. When his leathers become grimy through several months' wear, he will switch to a new set because he realises the importance of a neat appearance. Obviously, a contract with a leathers manufacturer who supplies the goods free does help!

Grant will also scrap a crash helmet if he comes off, even if there is no visible damage.

What's the point in taking a risk? I can't comprehend how some riders spend hundreds of pounds on gleaming machines but turn out in tatty leathers and old grazed crash hats that have seen better days. They have machines worth a lot of money but their helmets are so bad that the first time they fall off they wouldn't be fit to ride their bikes again.

All scrutineers should reject a helmet that shows a bad scrape. If a youngster can afford to go racing, he can afford to buy a high-standard polycarbonate helmet for little more than a crankshaft rebuild. By stopping a guy riding because his helmet has been rejected, a life might be saved.

Grant shudders at some of the tricks to which enthusiasm drove him and his colleagues in his early years. At scrutineering – those vital minutes when machines and equipment are checked for their suitability for racing – Grant would be sent away without the necessary permit to race because of side-to-side play in the back wheel of his Velocette due to the short life of its bronze swing arm. He would nip back to the paddock, tap the end of the swing arm bush with a centre punch to make it a snug fit and make the wheel stable enough to satisfy the scrutineers, who were always astounded at how quickly the bushes has been 'replaced'. Two laps later the wheel would be wobbling again, but Grant was in the race.

Experience makes you overcome this enthusiasm – for your own safety as much as anything. I am very safety-conscious because I

They appear to be mis-shapen when he stands upright, and it is only when he is seated on the machine in the racing position that the leathers closely hug his skin. They are so tailored that he has to unzip them before standing up. The leathers are kept supple by regular cleaning with saddle soap and the way to 'break in' a brand new set is to sit in them at home and to use them in short practice sessions until they fit perfectly.

For a long race in mid-summer, Grant will spurn a new set in preference to an old, comfortable suit. Most are lined with cotton to stop the colouring being transferred to the body, and most riders wear a tee-shirt underneath to deal with sweating. To combat the heat, Grant also has two zipper vents just below the shoulders to allow cool air to circulate around his back.

A two-piece suit, zipped together at the waist (the design is intended to cut replacement costs) never found much favour because of the risk of the zip bursting in a crash, as Barry Ditchburn painfully found out when he was thrown off his seized Kawasaki at Nogaro in France. Safety garments made with economy in mind have never paid off!

Grant has his leathers made with the zip on the inside of each ankle to minimise skin loss in a fall; on the outside, it might more easily burst open. Leathers covering the parts of the

don't want to hurt myself. But having those thoughts doesn't make you an inferior rider. Good riding is riding safely. If you fall off, you can't be riding well and the name of the game is to be sitting on the bike travelling as fast as you can when you pass under the chequered flag.

I know you can still get away with murder at scrutineering, as I did in the early days when I really hadn't the money to go racing. But the standard isn't bad considering those who do it are amateurs. I'd much rather the scrutineer check every nut and bolt of my machine than pass it through uninspected just because it's Mick Grant's bike.

Some scrutineers have come in for criticism but in the Isle of Man each year we have had a ludicrous situation where all petrol pipes must be wired onto the tank and carbs. The Japanese had gone to great lengths to add wire spring clips that are easy to remove with pliers yet won't work loose. The scrutineers at the TT insisted that these clips be wired, so it proved a devil of a job when it came to whipping carbs off quickly to change main jets.

Scrutineering overall could be more flexible but tougher. The chief scrutineer has a heavy burden to carry, especially if someone is killed and it comes out at the inquest that something wrong with the bike went unseen at scrutineering.

No matter what make of helmet Grant wears (like many of the top names, he has changed brands over the years), he insists on twin-riveted chin straps rather than a single rivet either side, so that it halves the risk of the helmet being ripped off in a crash. Of course, the helmet also has to be new.

As you become a professional, you find things come a lot easier. I don't have to pay £40 for a crash helmet. If I fall off I can get another one for nothing. I don't have to check to see if it's cracked or the inside has been damaged on impact and risk using it again – I change it. But I know a club lad couldn't always do that. It's the same with leathers: I can easily replace them with new ones, so I'm in a better position to be safety-conscious.

The full-face helmet now rules racing. A design which the sport's governing body once suggested should be banned because of the risk of breaking riders' necks, it is accepted as the safest form of headgear available in the sport. Technology has brought the helmet a long way from the days of the famous 'pudding basins' and Grant fancies there will be further improvements in the future.

Helmet development is always aimed at improving safety and in ten years' time we might scoff at today's designs.

To ensure his helmet remains a snug fit, he often puts in extra pieces of foam padding to tailor it comfortably to his head. It has to be firm as opposed to be tight. One difficulty which has plagued many riders since full-face helmets became the vogue is the misting up of visors on the inside caused by condensation. After trying every product on the market, Grant now swears by washing-up liquid. A few drops of the liquid rubbed on with a cloth keeps it clear of the mist caused by a rider's hot breath. The outside of the visor is polished with a silicone wax, such as Turtle Wax, and rain drops skate off when travelling at speed.

You have to be careful, though. Carol accidentally got some soap liquid onto the draught excluder between the visor and helmet before a race at Cadwell. I was dicing with Steve Machin when the heavens opened. The rain got on the draught excluder and turned the soap into bubbles which covered the visor and left me with a blurred vision of Steve.

Wind noise can also be a source of annoyance inside the helmet, sometimes to the point of being almost deafening. A number of riders use ear plugs. If the wind noise is very loud on a high speed circuit, Grant places wads of cotton wool over his ears to kill the sound.

Two tear-off visors is the ideal number to combat the splattering of insects during a race on a hot day. Any more than that distorts vision but the Isle of Man, being an individual case, often requires three 'tear-offs' on top of the normal Lexan visor. On a wet day, Grant dispenses with them altogether as the rain-drops tend to creep between the different layers.

The 'tear-offs', extremely flimsy films of plastic, are attached to the helmet by sticky tape with the release pull on the right of the helmet so the right-hand can remain on the throttle. Once unsecured, the wind whips it away.

In the Isle of Man there are few places where you can safely take it off; you wait until you get to one of the straights. Because of moths and other insects, I have had moments when my vision has been so impaired that it was dangerous to ride.

The Lexan visor – occasionally a tinted one depending on sun strength – is so tough that a ·22 air rifle pellet fired at point-blank range will not pierce it, so there is no danger of loose gravel being shot through from the rear tyre of a machine in front. Care has to be taken, though, if the 'tear-offs' are attached to the visor for a long period. A chemical reaction between the two different materials can cause the visors to crack, so that Grant will never build up his layers of sight protection the night before a race.

One thing that concerns me about all this sometimes is the rider on public roads who buys a tinted visor because he's seen a star using one. It will be OK in the daylight but the guy is in trouble if he wants to ride home in the dark. That's dangerous.

RIDING

From a riding point of view I've always considered myself as good as the best and better than most. You have to think that way, whether you're right or wrong. I don't think I've ever started a race without thinking I could win it, even if, on paper, I stood no chance.

At grand prix level it's important to weigh up every rider in your race and remember what they're capable of. You know from the past that some will go quicker in the race while others will go slower. Some might fly for perhaps 12 laps and then slow down through lack of stamina. Then there are those who go faster and faster and put in their best lap right at the end. There are so many permutations to consider that it is difficult to decide whether to clear off and try to build up a good lead, or to let someone else make the running. If you make a bad start, can you pull up or do you try merely to finish? Is it more important to finish or to have a go at winning for the sake of prestige and risk not finishing? Before the flag drops, your intentions should be quite clear – it's not all about going flat out from the start every time, as the public might think.

Some riders are notorious for putting in a very fast practice lap but being unable to match that performance in the race. Often, the reverse happens and riders in the race knock seconds off their best training time. On his first visit to the Czechoslovakian Grand Prix, Grant lapped seven seconds quicker in the 250 race than in practice.

British riders – brought up on meetings where they have no need to go exceptionally fast in practice because they have been seeded for the main race – find qualifying for grands prix difficult. This results in the average Briton struggling in practice but – remembering his UK habits – possibly going much quicker in the grand prix.

If riders are in the habit of using practice only to set up themselves and their bike, then they will have great difficulty in going quickly at grands prix training sessions. In practice for grands prix, you're racing against the clock; in the race, you're against other people.

One psychological ploy adopted by riders with bikes that have a speed advantage is to put in the quickest lap right at the very end of the final practice session, which can demoralise those who thought that practice times had settled into a pattern. The risk is that rain might fall in the final session. The

capable riders will only be happy with a place on the two front rows of the starting grid. The competition is so tough and evenly matched, that to be further back presents one with a near impossible task of getting through the pack. Even to pass one rider in a grand prix might take three laps – and those three laps could lose one a second per lap on the race leaders. The early leader with a clear road ahead has a big advantage; if he builds up a healthy margin between himself and the next rider, he has only to worry about being delayed by back markers or by those returning to the fray from the pits.

There's nothing worse than going out in front and having someone right behind you. They can judge your weak and strong points, but you can't get the same feed-back on them. A following rider will know where to pass you near the end of the race, which won't leave you time to weigh up his poor sections and maybe overtake him. It makes life so much easier to sit behind a guy: you can decide where he's best – it might be a case of him doing one corner better than you – and you copy him so as to be as good as him at that point. All that's left then are the stretches where you already know that you are better than him.

Riding styles among road racers vary enormously. While some assume a spectacular hang-off style, Grant prefers to sit directly over the machine with all extremities tucked in, because he believes it offers better control. Although each contrasting riding position has its devotees, the hang-off cornering style with the bottom out of the saddle – executed so brilliantly by American Kenny Roberts – does heighten the risk of the knees being scraped on the tarmac. Grant, however, only puts out his knees to obtain improved balance on corners in the wet, and where grip is at a premium.

If the bike gets into a wobble, you wouldn't think a hang-off rider would be in as strong a position to correct it as he would when sat over it. But it's all down to whatever style suits the rider best: personally, I never catch my knee on the floor unless I make a mistake. On the smaller bikes, the hang-off style has got to attract more wind resistance and therefore slow down the machine.

A team will work out the minimum amount of fuel to be carried to last the race. Over the years, machines have been lightened in every

opposite
Firmly in the saddle or hanging off the bike – whatever the style, both Grant and Sheene corner amazingly fast

way by manufacturers and so a surplus gallon of fuel carried throughout an event makes a mockery of their efforts and can affect handling. Grant gauges his to leave around half a gallon at the end of a race. It is not always possible to accurately assess how much fuel a bike will need for a given distance. Grant and his team had the embarrassing experience in the 1978 Junior TT of running out after two and a half laps when the tank was expected to last for three and a half; subsequent investigation revealed that insufficient fuel was put in at the start.

Most two strokes run on a 100 octane fuel mixture, although an adequate grade is not always available in some countries. Once, when a call was going out for riders to prepare for practice during the Spanish Grand Prix at Jarama, neither Grant's Kawasaki nor that of team-mate Kork Ballington would start. After considerable panic, the fault was diagnosed as lack of a special additive which allows the oil to be mixed with the petrol. The oil was sinking to the bottom, completely filling the carburettor float chambers. A drop of acetone-type fluid – a good marrying agent – cured the problem.

On race days, Grant rarely has more than a cup of tea for breakfast followed by a light lunch or maybe a sandwich. Only when the meeting is over will he sit down to a main meal. As long as he gets enough sleep to feel refreshed on the morning of a meeting, he is rarely worried about going to bed late the night before, unlike several top professionals who make a habit of retiring to their hotel rooms at an early hour.

Where riders are involved with push starts – the normal procedure in grands prix – most would want to set off on a straight course and be bang on the line for the first bend.

In many cases with a push start, it is better to be on the second row because, although many won't admit it, you do tend to anticipate the flag. Being one row back allows you to anticipate better than those on the front, because the starter has more of a job spotting you and because you can keep an eye on those on the front row. If any of them anticipate the flag, you can go with them.

The greatest problem faced by many riders of four cylinder machines when starting is to translate all that horsepower into usable power. The spectacular mono-wheeling, which delights crowds the world over, is unwelcome. Whenever the front wheel is punched high into the air, valuable seconds are lost while the power is rolled off to bring it back to earth. Grant reckoned his mighty Kawasaki was no speedier off the line than a big road bike because of the troublesome 'wheelie-popping'!

In first gear with the Kawasaki it was dead easy to get the front end up. The 680 Suzuki was capable of doing it in every gear, not only be-

cause of its engine performance but because of its balance and weight distribution. Wheelies are alright for the spectator and I enjoy doing them, but they can make or break a race if you have to back off the power to bring it under control.

The three-cylinder Kawasaki was a doddle to start but a big 1,000cc four cylinder bike weighs two or three hundredweight and might be a pig to push start. If they were left on the grid in a push start, it would be bad racing, so clutch starts are a must for big machines; it's far fairer and safer, too.

Clutch starts eliminate the problem in production racing where, in push starts, a rider can have his finger on the electronic starter button to give him an unfair advantage.

There has often been criticism of starters' flag-waving characteristics, which have not always been compatible with the demands of the modern, high-powered racing motorcycle. With clutch starts, and with many thousands of horsepower waiting to be unleashed from the grid, a starter can spoil a race just by twitching the flag before it is actually lowered to let them get away.

From an organiser's point of view, the conventional push start presents no major problem, although the flag-man has to have split second timing where the bigger machines are involved.

above
The quick-filler dump can fills a fuel tank in a matter of seconds

opposite, top
Gregg Hansford, pride of Australia

opposite, bottom
Steve Baker, in common with a number of top riders, prefers to hang off his machine when cornering

The old trick with dead engine starts was for the starter to slightly twitch the flag, which would encourage one or two into taking a couple of paces forward. He would then point to the offenders to order them back into their grid positions and, as they wheeled their bikes back, he'd drop the flag and catch them out. It was a bit of a game and most accepted the practice, whether they enjoyed it or not. But you cannot do that with clutch starts and 30 water-cooled bikes revving up in first gear.

The trouble is that many starters are unprofessional in their approach to the 750s. Instead of finding out why there has been a succession of false starts, some starters are interested only in ensuring that the riders obey their every command.

Many of the dyed-in-the-wool starters are so bent on getting precise lines of riders, just like battalions of soldiers, that they hold the bikes too long. The danger isn't so much that of burning out the clutch but of the engine boiling over, especially on a hot day. It's no secret that a water-cooled engine will often run better and give its maximum horsepower when several degrees below its normal running temperature. So I like to get on the track with the engine fairly cold and it will be just right after the warm-up lap. Any delay on the grid, however, and the engine will heat up and lose its edge.

A starter's job might seem very short – per-

haps only ten seconds – but to a rider it could be a lifetime. When everyone has returned from a warm-up lap, the starter should already be on his rostrum with the flag by his side. He should then nod to the guy with the 'engage gear' board to move off and within five seconds he should have his flag up and down. It's as easy as that, but some will never learn.

The green light starting system, which was adopted by a number of tracks in the mid-1970s, helped cut the likelihood of cheating, because it by-passed any human error.

But it does tend to make us appear like robots. Being somewhat sentimental, I prefer to see the starter with his flag, as it's more personal and gives racing a little more character.

In any form of start, front-row runners can often be surprised by rivals who have qualified with inferior practice times bursting through from the back.

If you finish up with a faster practice time than the guy who's coming from the back, you know he's not going to beat you. All he can do is annoy you by getting in front and possibly hold you up for several laps. Tracks in the United States employ startline judges, who watch for any creeping forward by riders, who may well be penalised for their misdemeanour. This leads to almost perfect starts.

But at the end of the day it's always going to be the same people who win the races, so I'm not sure that we need these judges in European racing. Really, there's very little controversy amongst riders about the starting methods of their rivals.

The best guys, the quickest, will always have the best machines and the best tackle. On equal machinery, they will win; on factory equipment, they will be even further in front. The secondary race is between the privateers and this will always be the case.

Grant feels that clutch starts – now used with only bigger-capacity machines – are safer, because a sick motor will see a rider away at half speed whereas someone unable to fire up his engine can become a victim of those coming through behind him, putting him at personal risk.

If Grant is not on the front row, he will often advise the two riders ahead of him that he intends to go through the gap between them; if they're friends and there is enough room, they will make space available for his rush.

At international meetings, where grid positions are less rigid, the clever rider who is not on the front row will always get himself behind someone he knows is a quick starter.

If it's a push start, it is always good to be behind Wil Hartog, because he's a ridiculously fast starter. He has the right physical size for push-starting and also has a good technique. Kenny Roberts, on the other hand, isn't particularly fast, while some of the big names are

bloody awful: you wouldn't want to find your-self behind Barry Sheene, for instance! A rider who has been given a front row position through a mistake in practice times, as happened with Gerhard Vogt in the 1977 British 750cc world championship round, is also a big handicap for those behind him. You'd make sure not to get behind him, because he just wouldn't be first away under normal circumstances.

Starting techniques, if efficiently executed, can win races and there is generally a basic formula for getting away cleanly from a push start. Spectators will often see a rider per-forming a little ritual prior to the flag being raised – checking that he's engaged first gear, that the petrol is switched on and that the engine is on its compression stroke or back off it, whichever is best for his machine. When the pack is allowed to surge away, a good style will work wonders.

Some grand prix riders drop the clutch, feed in the throttle and wait for the engine to pick up. It'll go plop-plop-plop then they'll pull in the clutch, rev it and get away. That's not the way to do it. With a 250 or 350 Yamaha (which has a 180 degree crank) you should push as fast as is needed to spin the engine, then let go of the clutch and immediately whip it back in again. When it has fired you have the advantage of no drag on the motor from the clutch and can freely rev up. The guys who drop the clutch and let it run plop-plop-plop cannot accelerate, be-cause the rear wheel has to be turned and, of course, a racing engine has no power at tick-over. By getting it fired and reducing that clutch drag, you can quickly rev up to get on the power.

Most racing bikes require two or three paces from the rider before firing, although Grant's 250cc and 350cc Grand Prix Kawa-saki twins had 360 degree cranks which (with the pistons firing together) made them like big single-cylinder motors, and these did require more effort. Riders may 'bump-start' the machine depending on the gear ratios.

If you try in practice to run with the bike and the back wheel doesn't skid once the clutch is released and pulled back in, then there would be no need to bump it.

The 750 Kawasaki he rode to many fine victories could be started immediately with-out requiring any weight on it from the rider. But too much throttle, leaving the clutch out for too long, not pushing the bike far enough, or sometimes just nerves are all reasons why riders may not be able to start first time – al-though they might have rehearsed the act per-fectly in the paddock a dozen times before the race.

Fouled plugs were once an explanation for not starting but the warm-up lap now cleans up any oiling, while modern electrics give such an intense spark at the bottom end that, even with a wet plug, an engine will normally fire.

The rider with long legs and a small bike will clearly be keen to 'paddle' his machine away, a practice Grant prefers unless his machine needs a hard bump. For hours on end, Grant experimented with his single cylinder racers at the beginning of his career to perfect the most successful techniques.

The old style involved sitting side-saddle once it was started and, when it had reached 40 mph or so, the rider's leg would be cocked over the bike. But it has been proved that the modern way of getting astride the bike straight away is far better. The old singles did not have the thrust to pop wheelies, so it was safe to sit side-saddle. Do that on a modern twin and you've no control over it. Anyway, the most spectacular starter is not necessarily the quickest. Like any skilled worker, the guy who makes it look easy and unspectacular is very often the one who's doing it the best.

Grant uses the racing lines taken by fellow competitors to find his way round a fresh track. If he doesn't know the right lines, he will watch them closely to discover the correct way.

The biggest single lesson I ever learned was at Croft in the very early days. There was a chap called Tom Armstrong, one of the top nor-thern riders. He happened to sneak out on a 250cc Aermacchi in a 500cc practice session. My 500cc Velocette would just about hang on to his 250 over four laps of Croft. I didn't know what racing was about until I followed him. It really opened my eyes. He went from white line to white line, from one side of the circuit to the other at each corner, using every inch of the road. His corners were nine feet wider than mine, so he was going through them ten miles an hour faster than me.

Almost certainly, every top professional has learned a similar lesson during his early development. If there is an inch of tarmac to spare on the track, the good rider will use it. By gaining six inches on entry to a bend and a further six on exiting, he has a valuable extra foot to enable him to go through that much faster.

Copying is one way of getting on in this busi-ness. I've always been a copier. While natural ability will give you the right racing lines where-ever you go, I found the correct lines through experience and by watching and copying. Occasionally, I've become lazy and have had to jog myself into tidying up my lines. If I'm passed in a race when I know I shouldn't be, due to sloppiness on my part, I make certain I get back on the right racing line, even if it means watching the line of the guy in front.

Braking should allow the power to be fed in early coming out of a corner. That's why, when an individual is riding bang on form, some might think he has a very quick engine; in actual fact, he's putting the power on five or ten yards earlier than the rest leaving a corner. So

he has an extra distance of acceleration to use when getting onto the straight. Road racing's all about accelerating and not so much about braking.

If you're leading in a tidy manner and there's no-one in the way, all you're fighting is the clock. It stands to reason that if the leader's average lap times are better than anyone else's, he will win the race. Quite often, a passing manoeuvre will lead to a slower lap time, because overtaking the guy in front might involve taking a completely different line to outbrake him into a corner. That puts you on a different angle exiting from the bend and so makes you slower onto the straight. But at least the slower guy has been passed and the next guy can be caught up.

If you're leading or are in a position where there is nobody holding you up, then you must make the quickest possible lap (which perhaps sounds like common sense). If you're lying behind someone you want to pass, then fast lapping has to be forgotten and all that's in your mind is to get past that guy somehow. That used to be the difference between grand prix racing and short circuit scratching. In England, they run such short races that you're always having to pass people; it doesn't matter about stringing together 80 miles of neat, fast riding to get a ten-second advantage, as is needed in GPs.

The English technique at somewhere like Gerard's Bend at Mallory would be to approach it as fast as possible, brake like hell, throw the bike on its side and scrape round. The grand prix technique was always to go in hardly touching the brakes; by going much more smoothly, the bike would not wobble, while taking an outside, wider, deeper line, made the corner much bigger, so that you'd come out ten miles an hour quicker from the bend. When scratching, you'd be on the inside line, trying to get past the next man, making you slower all the way round and slower coming onto the straight. The total effect is that the GP runner would be 30 yards ahead of the scratcher on the straight following the corner. Apart from Silverstone, however, there is nowhere in England where you would have to use the GP technique.

Racing now has become more universal and all the techniques seem to have blended together, but in the old days I could lap someone like Chas Mortimer at Brands, but he would see me off in a grand prix.

Geoff Duke used to say that you should go into a corner slowly and come out fast but I don't think he phrased it right. What he should have said was: 'Go into a corner in complete control as quickly as you can and come out faster'. It's much more important to come out of a corner fast than to go into it fast and the

Flying Dutchman Wil Hartog on the 680cc Suzuki

47

right
Even superstars have heart-stopping moments, as Barry Sheene proves when chasing Pat Hennen. Sheene somehow managed to correct this wicked rear slide!

right
Grant takes ex-British Champion Roger Marshall

opposite
Follow my leader: Barry Sheene heads the best of the 500cc grand prix contenders, each one seeking a tow from the rider ahead

48

longer the straight after the corner, the more important that corner is. A corner which leads onto a straight has to be entered so that you can put the power on ten yards earlier than the guy ahead when coming out onto the straight. One hundred yards up that straight, you will be going quicker than a guy whose bike has the same horsepower.

Riders slipstreaming one another is a common sight and Grant considers it fair play to move the machine about to break the following rider's tow.

When they're wiggling about you do tend to think it might be a dangerous operation to attempt to pass them. I know of riders who will follow your tail for half the distance and just as you think they'll be coming through at any second, you look round and find they've dropped several seconds back. Then there are those who are like bulldogs and will never give up. If you know the guy behind is going to win the race because of his superior machinery, there's little you can do about it. What can throw you is to look behind and see an unrated runner there.

Because the leading rider always has the choice of line, the sport accepts blocking tactics, where one rider closes the way through on another.

It is most infuriating when riders block you when you're coming through from a bad start. A few riders will do that, holding you back for a couple of laps, for no reason at all other than their warped competitive spirit. They know from the outset that they have no chance of actually beating you.

Some riders are ruthless and others are very fair. Cheating and rough-riding might help someone to take a few short cuts in his career, but the person with ability will always win through.

The two-wheeled trouble-maker often finds himself being overtaken rather too closely for comfort, while those with honest reputations are always given a respectable margin of width.

Racing is a calculated risk; it's always a question of trying to establish what the limits are. But it's much nicer to pass somebody and not interfere with their riding, although it's not always possible to do that. The easiest way to overtake a rider is on the inside and it's the safest, too, when a guy with a reputation for crashing is being passed. If they do fall off and you're on the inside, there's no chance of you being taken with them.

Braking hard into a tight corner, the experienced rider will feel little sensation: with his arms braced against the handlebars, he has encountered the feeling many times before. It therefore comes as a surprise to hear Grant confess that, while fierce acceleration and braking, and the bucking or even sliding of the bike, leave him unmoved, a trip up a high

building or a ride on a funfair 'big dipper' bring on a queasy sensation he finds hard to deal with!

Back on the track, however, one of the hardest situations to cope with is an S-bend taken at high speed.

Going round a left-hander really fast, you naturally have to put some weight on the right. It's all down to the gyroscopic forces and can give you a super sensation. Somewhere like Bishopscourt in the Isle of Man, going almost flat-out in top, you have to press the bars right to go round the left-hander and then attempt to pull the wheel to the left for the following right-hand bend. You are literally pulling it in the opposite direction, holding the bars hard to prevent them from going too far over. The big bikes certainly do require some manhandling in that sort of situation.

Like many riders, Grant never uses the clutch going up through the gears because it allows a smoother change. Unless he is in a terrific hurry, however, he uses it when changing down. Going through from first to sixth, the right revs would be reached and, as

the throttle is eased back, the pedal is nicked into the next gear. It's a much more silky procedure than if the clutch was operated.

Changing down, I find I cannot blip the throttle and snick down a gear without being brutal, so I use the clutch.

There are still occasions when I would use the clutch changing up, on an adverse camber, for instance, where you have to change gear on the corner and the bike is just beginning to slide a little.

Tradition has encouraged a vast number of riders to ride with a couple of fingers on the clutch lever but Grant feels that seizures – the reason for doing it – are a thing of the past. Only if the temperature gauge recorded a boiling 105 degrees or broke because of the bike's vibration would he place a couple of precautionary fingers on the lever, but he thinks it far more important to have both hands in full control of the bike.

Of all the malfunctions the one I dread most is the gearbox locking when, even after pulling in the clutch, the rear wheel will be solid. A piston seizure normally happens when you're

The waterproof oversuit keeps out at least some of the rain and so helps make racing in these conditions at least a bit more bearable, as Grant demonstrates during the 1973 Hutchinson

knocking off the power at the end of a straight and you'll often catch it without falling off. But if a circlip comes off and jams two or three gears together, brother, you'd be in bother because the clutch would not unlock the back wheel. That is a frightening thought. Another fear of mine is tyre failure on high speed circuits, something which can pitch you off in a flash before you can take any evading action. Any malfunction where there is a chance of catching it if you're quick enough doesn't unduly bother me.

Most youngsters today have the gear-change pedal on the left, because mass-produced road machines are constructed that way. Grant prefers his on the opposite side – where all bikes once had them – although he is right-handed for everything except writing, which he does with his left hand.

Aerodynamics play a vital role in raising a motorcycle's top speed, especially on fast circuits. Grant felt that the large Kawasaki fibreglass fairing on his 750 triple might be over-bulky, so he once experimented in the Isle of Man with a fairing from the rival RG

Rider's-eye view of the two dials that a road racer must keep a watchful eye on – the rev counter and the temperature gauge

Look at that fairing! Italian ace Carlo Ubbiali pilots his 250cc MV Agusta to another Lightweight TT win in 1956

500 Suzuki. He found that the more pointed Suzuki streamlining did not suit the Kawasaki – it cost him 15 seconds over the lap, and pushed up the water temperature.

In wet conditions, where the clear perspex 'bubble' is obscured with rain drops, the rider will raise his eye-line above the screen, but aerodynamics have proved that a helmet protruding over the top in that manner makes no vast difference. Under hard braking, a rider will sit up, not only to increase wind resistance but also to re-distribute the body weight over the rear wheel and prevent it from lifting.

The small, foam-padded seat provides little comfort but the rider's full weight is often on the footrests (as he manoeuvres the machine) or on the tank, as he lays flat behind the fairing on the fast stretches.

When he first raced in the TT, Grant's stomach took such a buffeting from the tank on the Sulby Straight that he felt physically sick. On the same section with the Kawasaki some years later, there was no pain because he was flying over the bumps where before he was going through them at almost half the speed.

Occasionally, you can get knocked out of the saddle and onto the tank: that can really make your eyes water! It takes a few deep breaths to get you back into the rhythm again.

Handling is, of course, assisted by the hydraulic damper protruding from one end of the handlebars. The adjustment – there are six settings – is normally made in the paddock, but riders of Grant's calibre will turn the knurled screw during a race to get improved steering.

On the softest setting, there is almost no indication of the bike having a damping system; with the firmest setting, it's quite difficult even to turn the bars from lock to lock. When handling problems with the 750cc Kawasaki caused some anxiety in the 1975 TT he had the damping on the stiffest setting, forcing him to put his feet down at the tight Governor's Bridge because he could not turn the handlebars quickly enough. The hydraulic system – Grant usually favours a medium setting – superseded the familiar friction damper which was considered by many to be rather ineffective at high speed.

Riding different-sized machines is not as difficult as spectators might imagine. Practice makes perfect and Grant, like many capable competitors, has raced several capacities in one afternoon and won each time. A rider can quite easily adjust to a variety of machines and to their particular characteristics, provided he is not away from one class of machine for too long.

I got back onto a 750 after riding a 250 for

most of the time, and nearly fell off three times in as many laps because I was going too deep into corners before braking. That was dangerous, but if you're changing bikes all the time, there should be no problem making the transition. But people are tending not to race in four classes these days. That's due to the expense more than the desire to specialise in certain classes.

Although the days when some riders would enter as many as three classes in grands prix are gone, because of a ruling restricting competitors to a maximum mileage at a world championship round, successful short circuit racing in several classes is still possible.

I find it most distressing when I've only had one race all day. It's far better to be over-raced than under-raced, because that leads to a lack of practice on a particular track and denies you the opportunity to sharpen yourself up. You also tend to have too much time on your hands, which allows mental pressure to build up. By having just one race, which might end in a breakdown, the whole meeting can be a one hundred per cent failure. Three or four rides on different machines increase the chance of a good runner having some success. A couple of successful races that day will mean a happy weekend and a share of the press the following week.

But where does courage and daring come in? Surely, these must be essential attributes for anyone considering racing at over 180 mph on two wheels and in competition with other determined men?

That's where people are completely wrong. I've got a big yellow stripe up my back. I'm a coward and I don't mind admitting it; deep down, there are one or two others who would judge themselves in more or less the same way. There are no bold, old riders. My days of riding wildly on the limit lasted a couple of seasons. It was a hairy patch we all go through. After that comes confidence in your own ability and the biggest coward in the world who possesses confidence will still succeed. I certainly don't want to fall off, I don't like hurting myself and I try not to. It's seventy per cent confidence and perhaps thirty per cent courage. That confidence can be split into different areas – confidence in knowing that the start money you have organised is right, confidence in your machine, in your mechanics and in your own ability.

Coming from a man who has gone round the Isle of Man Mountain circuit – arguably the world's most demanding – at all-time record speeds, it may come as a shock to hear him say he is a coward.

It's got me out of bother more than once. A cautious start to build up confidence works for me, and I tend to get quicker and quicker each time. When I was learning speedway, it took me ages just to slide the bike, but there are

people who can slide a machine first time out. I couldn't do that – it's not in my make-up. I don't get instant results. In my first season, I wasn't one of these guys who had the proud distinction of achieving a win. Not having this immediate skill to win hasn't done me any harm – it has just taken me that bit longer to get to the top.*

But even Grant passed through a wild stage where risks were taken. He used to be regularly accosted by a worried spectator, who pleaded with him not to ride because he was convinced that Grant was going to do himself harm.

But I savour the old days. I recall when Ken Redfern used to talk about this black-leathered figure on a black motorbike who would slither alongside him at the Croft hairpin. That was me being inexperienced and wild!

Phil Haslam was one rider, Grant reckons, whose wild patch lasted a lot longer than most other people's. But the untimely death of such a promising rider (at Scarborough) came at a time when he was over this erratic spell and was riding much more comfortably.

The South African, Dudley Cramond, went through this difficult phase, when he was criticised for bringing people off. But I sympathised with him, because I know we all go through it. I've fetched people off on occasions and I wouldn't want to sign a piece of paper guaran-

Dunce's hat for Grant after he parted company with his bike in front of an interested gallery

teeing that from now until the end of my career I wouldn't bring anyone else off because of some mistake I had made. It's part of the game and, as long as you're not doing it frequently or deliberately, it has to be accepted. If riding errors are highlighted at international level, people are going to take notice. The only way people like Cramond can get through that patch is to get the racing mileage and the vital experience. Men in that position can finish up two ways: they either settle down or they hurt themselves. Whichever way, the sport won't suffer because they'll either be out of it or they'll be riding like model professionals.

Thinking about crashing helps you not to fall off and it would be a stupid rider who didn't consider the possibility of coming off. But I'm not frightened about going racing and I'm not frightened about going to the TT and killing myself. When your number's up, it's up. I'm still putting myself at risk if I go trials riding or just shopping in the high street.

During a bad run in the early part of the 1978 season, as he struggled to recapture his form and to overcome a series of mechanical failures, Grant came adrift from his Kawasakis several times in rapid succession. Throughout this traumatic period, crashing filled his thoughts, but he accepts that the average racer will take a tumble perhaps twice a season, through trying too hard as much as anything.

When I go round, I'm thinking that I mustn't fall off, rather than wondering if I'm going to come off through going too fast at a certain point. At most corners, you're too busy to do anything apart from concentrating on the tyres and the engine.

Courage, according to Grant, is only a very small part of a racing man's make-up, and then it can sometimes be mistaken for lack of experience.

Courage in an experienced rider is rare. To do something courageously is to do something in the unknown, as is often shown by youngsters without any real racing apprenticeship. When Sheene crashed at Daytona and came back seven weeks later at Cadwell, that was courage. Foolish, yes. Had he come off at Cadwell, they'd never have been able to piece him together again, but it was brave of him – and he had the experience to know better.

So, I'm a coward, I don't like falling off through mistakes. It hurts. But if I wasn't a fatalist, I'd be so terrified of falling off that I couldn't possibly get on a bike. At the same time, I think you can make your own luck. If I want to be the top motorcyclist, I have as much chance as the next man of being the top one. And broadly speaking, if I wanted to be a millionaire, I'd have as much chance as the next guy.

Throughout their careers, racers are lucky to escape without at least one major spill, but the good men always seem to get away relatively unscathed. Grant came adrift of his 750 Kawasaki at 150 mph at Ontario in the United States.

It was the same year as Sheene's monumental prang and was caused by the same fault – a burst tyre.

Coming off the banking and accelerating through fifth gear, Grant had just put his head on the tank for the straight when the whole machine was rocked by a sensational bang. His first thought was that the crank had snapped.

As he grabbed at the clutch, thinking it might be a broken crank, Grant's Kawasaki slewed sideways, the back end went up and flicked him into the air.

It was the feeling everyone must have experienced when they fall – it was like a slow motion effect as I came off. The mind works at twice the normal speed and therefore makes everything appear to happen slowly. It seems an awful long time before you hit the floor.

I can remember going backwards through the air head-first and seeing the sky from about seven feet up. I thought: 'Shit, this is going to hurt'. I reckoned it would be the last time I would fall off a motorbike.

He floated through the air until he hit the tarmac, then slid feet-first behind the tumbling bike, which he could still see. He was then thrown back onto his feet and found himself running, some say at over 60 mph.

He finally landed in a heap, grateful to be still in one piece. Apart from a selection of burns, scratches and bruises, his injuries did not even require hospitalisation.

It proves that so much depends on fate. I could have really hurt myself, but I was out testing bikes at Riverside the following day. Now it's an incident that has almost been forgotten. The only occasions I retell the story are at club dinners and at forums, when I'm invariably asked about my worst crash – they always ask that of any top racer. But it was just a small incident. You only look back on such things if you're lacking in confidence. Racing is all about going forwards, not backwards and your thoughts should be in the same direction as the bike is heading.

The best rides are always those which the rider enjoys. But after a series of unexplained crashes, it takes time to restore confidence. Once the cause is discovered, however, there is no reason why anything should detract from a rider's performance. Grant suffered two successive mystery spills in 1978 followed by a third where he was again blameless, but he returned to his best form within a matter of weeks once the cause had been established. He has had only one mishap which still remains a mystery: chasing Tony Rutter flat out on a 350 Yamaha round Chapel Curve at Silverstone, Grant caught the first slide but not the second, which pitched him over the bars. There was no oil on the track and the bike had not seized.

There must have been an explanation, but I never found one and that's worrying because, if you don't know the reason, you don't know when it will happen again.

What that accident taught him was never to wear lightweight boots again. He was using sidecar racer's boots with a flat, vulcanised sole without a heel. The crash ripped off the sole and, seconds later, removed the rest of the boot.

Race fans throughout the world have wondered what goes through the mind of a racer about to crash. Grant knows the feeling – and the action needed to be taken.

Before I hit the deck, all I'm thinking about is hoping that I won't hurt myself, but you have to deal with the situation as it evolves. The first part to bother about is landing. If you're sliding along the ground at a great rate of knots, you're looking for what you might hit. Once that danger has passed, a glance around might be made for bikes coming up behind. People say the text-book way to fall, which is absolute bull-shit, is to roll up into a ball. But when you roll, you start to break things. The ideal way is to be flat on the back with arms and legs out wide like a starfish so that weight distribution prevents any one part of the body from taking all the abrasion. When flat-out, you'll be most unlucky if you break anything.

It's survival instinct that matters. At some time in their life, a person driving a car has had to make a snap decision over which way to go in a crisis. Almost invariably, the right choice is made. If you went through the same situation afterwards with diagrams and photographs, you might choose the other way but your decision has to be made in that split second – and it's often the right choice.

If there is an ideal condition for falling off, it has to be wet weather, when a sliding rider has only a small risk of hurting himself on a friction-free surface. An abrasive track surface which tears through leathers is the enemy of the dislodged rider. At Brands Hatch, where there is hardly any grip for bikes in wet weather, a fallen rider might not even scuff his leathers.

On a smooth surface, I'd much sooner fall off on the track than onto the grass run-off areas. If you're heading towards the grass, there's a risk of hitting a raised kerb, which really hurts if you're flat on your back. I've always said the old grippy surface in the Isle of Man was the best. Now the new, smooth surface which holds the damp stops you from finding the limit of your control over the bike. When there was a bumpy surface of granite chippings, the bike shook about a lot, leaving a wide safety margin between racing on the limit and crashing. With the present-day shiny black surface, the first

indication of over-stretching your limit is a sideways slide.

Whatever circuit owners may think, track-side safety precautions are unsympathetic to motorcycle racers. Armco barriers, erected purely for car racing, are no help to the man protected only by a leather uniform and a crash helmet; even when these steel fences are adequately cocooned by straw bales they can still be a misery for the two-wheeled exponent.

If the bales are enclosed in polythene bags to prevent them from getting wet, then they're a better bet than Armco. But on circuits where the bales are exposed to rain, the Armco might just as well be left unprotected. Wet bales serve no useful purpose. Although it's much more expensive, the ideal situation would be the use of plastic, foam-filled bags everywhere. With occasional patching up of holes, they would last a long time and, for me, they are a far better proposition. But I know it must be easier for circuit bosses to go to a farmer once a year, agree a price and bring in piles of straw bales.

All road racers would agree with Grant when he suggests that the ideal short circuit has a 30-yard run-off area at each corner, with the Armco set back, but a shortage of room makes this impossible at some places.

If a motorcyclist is going to crash, the first thing he wants to do is to get off the bike. This was really brought home to me when I was right

After fuel on the rear tyre put his motorcycle into a spin, Grant comes adrift in front of pursuers Dave Potter (2) and Ron Haslam during the North-West 200 in Northern Ireland

55

Avoiding action is often necessary, as Grant painfully shows at Austria's Salzburgring, where he has taken to the grass to miss a rider pushing his machine on the bend, with unfortunate consequences

behind Kim Newcombe when he was killed at Silverstone. He kept struggling to control his sliding bike for a long way; had he realised he was going to hit something, he would still be alive today if he had jammed on the rear brake and got off the machine.

During one Austrian Grand Prix, Grant knew he had to part company with his 350 Kawasaki when a rider pushing his machine appeared on a blind bend directly in his path. As he took to the grass he realised that by remaining on the machine he would be catapulted with the bike off a ramp and into the crowd. To avoid possible mayhem, he slammed on the rear brake and laid the machine down.

If there's no way to ride it out, get off it. When a car touches the Armco in a slide, it might just put that vehicle back on course. That, I imagine, is the thinking behind having Armco, but the needs are vastly different for motorcycle racers. We only want Armco to prevent out-of-control bikes from going into the crowd at certain sections.

Catch-fencing, of course, is a safety feature many would like to see introduced on tricky corners. Silverstone is one of the few circuits to have the rows of 'chicken wire' erected at a bike meeting and many riders have been grateful for it. The safety-conscious Imola circuit in Italy is noted for its use of catch fencing, although Grant feels it loses its advantages when the supporting poles are made of angle iron!

I'm afraid it will always be Armco unless the car world decide that catch fences are better. The first time I crashed into a fence was at Paul Ricard in France at 120 mph. I couldn't believe how little damage had been done to my Kawasaki. Had there not been dirt in the carburettors, I could have ridden the thing back to the pits. But we motorcyclists are a weak body in that we don't get together to sort out such safety matters.

Personally I would sooner see a circuit kept on, even if the geography of the place prevented improvements from being made. We need more circuits, not less. If a boxer gets a smack on the nose in the ring, he knows it's to be expected. If I fall off and hurt myself in the Isle of Man because of the nature of the circuit, I know the risks.

Of the sport's danger spots, high on Grant's list comes Devil's Elbow, the left-hand kink at Mallory Park, where riders almost kiss the Armco at great speed. He has tumbled there once and counts himself lucky to be able to recall the incident.

Any circuits that can be made safer should be improved; the circuits which pass through a village or by someone's garden wall, where improvements are not possible, must be accepted for what they are. If some don't want to ride there, then they don't have to. But to see people

hurt at circuits where alterations could have been made does upset me.

While criticism can be levelled against the physical aspects of many circuits throughout Europe on various safety factors, fault can also be found with the human organisation at race meetings. Some track marshals in particular fall some way short of acceptable standards when required to act in emergencies.

I have video tapes in which marshals are seen dragging a fallen rider off the circuit or who have left their flag post to rush over to a bike. In general, marshalling is very good, but some do more harm than good. No matter how bad the situation is at the time, a marshal would do far more good waving his flag than by trying to help a crashed rider.

Grant feels that if the flag system is operated correctly there should be no danger to a crashed rider from following bikes. A well-organised event means a rider will never see the face of a flag marshal, whose controlling territory is always in the stretch of track between him and the next flag-point.

If an accident occurs two feet behind the marshal's back, that's nothing to do with him. He should still look in the direction the bikes are going. If the system is properly adhered to, that fallen guy is best left on the track until medical aid arrives.

Quite clearly, the better educated in racing ways the marshals are the safer it would help make the sport, although the days of professional marshals are some way off, especially for non-international meetings. The marshals, of course, can retort by saying that some riders act unprofessionally, as when waved warning flags are ignored by a few riders eager to take advantage of their rivals slowing down in accordance with the rules.

It's human nature and almost forgivable if there's a rider ahead whom you're dicing with and you can gain two or three yards on him as a result of a yellow flag being put out. But as soon as people are seen passing under the yellow flag and there's evidence to prove it, they should be automatically excluded from the rest of the meeting. Certain riders habitually do it. I wouldn't slow down under a motionless yellow flag, but you can immediately spot the marshalling points where a crash has occurred and, with the flags being waved, I'd then slow down.

What can be confusing to riders in wet conditions is the similarity of marshal's and photographer's red or amber waterproof jackets to warning flags. In the poor visibility, it can be hard to differentiate in a split second.

Stopping a race because of a serious crash has caused problems in the past, when it has proved difficult for a clerk of the course to communicate simultaneously with all marshalling points. A system at Scarborough used loud klaxons to instruct all marshals to put out their red flags to halt racing and this is

The Mallory Park hairpin, where bikes can go out of control at over 100 mph. Grant would like to see a run-off area here

an idea which Grant would like to see adopted at all circuits.

Less efficient marshals occasionally leave their flags curled up on the ground. The few seconds it would take to unfold them could be enough time for a bad accident to take place.

But I'm not knocking these guys. They do the job for nothing and we should be grateful to them for turning up at all.

While some might feel not all circuits throughout the world have adequate medical facilities to cope with today's high-speed injuries, Grant is satisfied that enough is generally done to take care of mishaps. But he suggests that medical attention should be left to those trained to carry it out.

A lot more damage is caused by marshals doing something they shouldn't rather than leaving an injured rider where he is. Over-enthusiasm is often a problem. OK, if a guy is face down being sick into his helmet, get the crash-helmet off at once, but for the rest of the time leave him until qualified help turns up.

Grant remembers one example of a marshals' enthusiasm to help which caused him a great deal of pain. After crashing at the Salzburgring, his leg was trapped underneath his bike. The excited marshals removed the machine and, unable to understand Grant's anguished cries that his ankle felt broken,

four of them lifted him further along the grass to a place they considered safer. Had his ankle suffered a complicated break, this could have had serious consequences, but it was just an automatic reaction by marshals keen to be seen doing their job.

Whenever Grant comes off his bike, he prefers to lay quietly for ten seconds to ascertain whether any bone is broken. Damage is often done by riders struggling to their feet on injured limbs instead of waiting to receive treatment.

If you're laid there, conscious and collecting yourself, the nicest thing is for a marshal to come along, maybe help you to remove your helmet and allow you to tell him what is wrong. A bit of plain sense instead of over-reaction should be the first move by a marshal.

The Japanese rider, Sadeo Asami had cause to remember the way he was handled by a Brands Hatch marshal who acted on impulse. Nursing a broken collar bone, he was sitting well out of danger until a keen marshal picked him by his injured arm and carried him away. Not being able to speak English, Asami was put through agony.

All riders consider it a priority to have good medical facilities on hand although motorcycle racing has still, in many countries, been unable to command an emergency helicopter to transport the injured to major hospitals.

Obviously, there is room for improvement but it has to be said that the general level of medical facilities is first class. I would like to see more qualified doctors involved but rather than digging our heels in, as has happened in the car world, let's be grateful for what we have already.

With blood pumping from a burst artery after a collision with a barrier, Grant once rode up to a marshalling point where the youngster on duty turned white at the sight of such an injury. As the marshal froze, Grant had to ride on to seek urgent attention at the medical centre.

On another occasion in Venezuela, after a minor prang in which Grant merely cut his hand, the under-worked ambulance crew refused to drop him off at the pits and rushed him to hospital three miles away.

It went across a ploughed field at a speed that would have certainly have finished me off had I been dying. Even though I banged on the cab to make him slow down, the driver wouldn't listen. Maybe he couldn't hear above the sounds of the old Coca-Cola cans rolling around inside the ambulance. There seemed to be more chance of being infected inside the wagon than lying injured in the open.

After having his wound dressed, Grant wanted to return to the San Carlos circuit, but there was no-one available to chauffeur him. So in just his underpants and a pair of white socks, he successfully hailed a passing ambulance which was returning to the track!

One danger aspect of modern-day motorcycle road racing is the proximity of some of the crowds to the action, especially in Europe where fans often do battle with police to get closer to their heroes. If it's safe to do so, however, Grant is in favour of having spectators near to the racing.

There can be nothing more boring than watching from 40 yards away as would be the case if the Armco was pushed back to make the ideal circuit. People won't pay to watch if we're specks of dust in the distance. Without people the circuit will be lost, so a happy balance has to be found.

Grant feels that all the British tracks are safe from a rider's viewpoint, apart from Mallory where modifications ought to be made to the hairpin, but he considers more spectators would go to Oulton Park in Cheshire if there were better viewing facilities.

Grant, the first active rider to be elected to the ACU Road Race Committee and to get involved in track inspection, also admits to 'getting the shudders' every time he arrives at Snetterton's hairpin at the end of the long, fast Norwich Straight.

With safety it's important always to have an open mind and to look at any suggestions which are put forward. You must not be frightened of making changes if they're for the better.

Some riders who have overdone it will attribute the blame for a crash to a fault with the bike and they will return to the paddock to tell their mechanics what is not right with the machine.

It is important to have an honest understanding with your mechanics and if they have made a mistake I expect them to admit it. Conversely, I hope I would be big enough to admit to any error.

Grant once spent a week worrying why he was thrown off his machine only to discover that his team manager knew but did not want to say, in case the mechanic – who had wrongly fitted the disc brake which caused the accident – became upset. Grant has also been on bikes that have seized through being jetted down by mechanics, who would still not admit to doing it afterwards.

You must be honest with yourself. There are times when you might say something to the press tongue in cheek, either to try and physche out an opponent or just for a bit of fun, but as long as you don't finish up believing it, no harm will come of it. If a rider error is to blame for a fall, I feel you must admit it and not, as a factory sometimes asked me to do, put the blame down to one of the standard list of excuses such as a patch of oil or a seizure. These little white lies might take the heat off for a while but, if you start believing they are the real reasons, the mental situation begins to get dangerous.

Just as insurance companies become more humane with their premium demands when drivers reach 26, so Grant reckons bike racers come to fruition around that age, after the sufficient experience has been gained.

If the lessons learned can be put into practice, there will be fewer mistakes and that's when you become more successful. Take Johnny Cecotto. He finally came through his wild period, and is now a much better rider. Even with the greatest courage in the world and the most enthusiasm, you cannot beat experience, as Hailwood proved on his return to racing in 1978. He had no intention of falling off and hurting himself. If the switch in the head is still on and you're still receptive, you'll be OK no matter what your age, because it isn't a physical sport. Still be hungry at 40 and you'll want to carry one. But some can get a taste for the easy life and racing can make them too cushy. From suddenly being hungry, they realise they don't want to spoil a good thing by falling off, so they try less hard. As long as you can fend off that feeling, you'll stay competitive. I don't think I would want to carry on racing if I was no longer competitive. Once that edge has gone, I would want to be doing something else in life, even if the absence of the sport left me frustrated.

Money is obviously an important considera-

Grant (750cc Kawasaki)
fights off a determined
challenge from Sheene
(650cc Suzuki)

opposite, bottom
American Steve Baker,
surprisingly dropped by
the Yamaha factory team
after finishing runner-up
in the 500cc world
championship in 1977

following page
Giacomo Agostini claimed
world championship titles.
He is pictured on a 350cc
MV Agusta at the
Italian Grand Prix

tion for any professional sportsmen, but it could never be the driving force as far as I'm concerned and I think you would find that applies to most of today's racers. On numerous occasions, I've won a race and looked very disappointed when I returned to the paddock, which some people find hard to understand. I've perhaps had more satisfaction from finishing seventh or eighth in a race, knowing I've done the job properly. Take 1978 for example, which was a bad season for me; I knew in my own heart that I was riding well, even though I wasn't able to get too many wins. If I know I'm riding as well as I can and as well as the machine allows me to, then I am as happy as a sandboy.

The hardest thing in the world must have been for Agostini to win as often as he did on an MV Agusta that was 20 mph faster than the Nortons at the time. I couldn't have done that. Competition brings me on and lack of it would bring me down. For Agostini to have no competition for so many years and still win so convincingly was absolutely incredible, but he had a personal standard to aim at and you have to admire him for keeping up that standard. The average guy on a 500 MV at the time would have been dicing with the fastest Nortons because his riding would have become so lazy. It's human nature to be forced into going quicker, as happened to me when Jarno Saarinen did the British international meetings. I suddenly found that instead of dicing with people like Tony Rutter, I could actually finish 30 seconds in front of him and two or three seconds behind Jarno. It's easy to be pulled out of yourself but to stay in front of those who are not quite so good is much harder. This is what personal achievement is about and that's why it's more important than winning. It will keep you competitive and prevent you becoming despondent because you aren't winning. I'm not saying you accept second but it's definitely not the end of the world. I knew a factory rider who came in from a fabulous race at Silverstone and said: 'Second isn't good enough for me'. Well I'm afraid at times it's good enough for the best of us and, to me, his was the wrong attitude. If he rode his best and felt he couldn't ride any better, then second should have given him as much satisfaction as first.

I'm not saying my approach is shared by all other riders. They are a bunch of individuals with differing outlooks and someone like Sheene may never be satisfied with second place. But it's clear you should always be aiming at a level higher than the one you're at – you're better finishing in the first half dozen at an international than winning a national. Aim for the toughest competition there is. The harder the opposition the more I like it.

When Grant rode at club level, the name Steve Jolly usually spelt defeat for all those who tried to battle against him but, because

Jolly spent far too long at that level, he found it almost impossible to move into higher categories successfully.

Lack of competition can definitely make you go soft. It's so important to spend the right number of years at each stage, but still know when to up-grade yourself.

Proof of the fact that racing – whether on two or four wheels – is not a physical sport was shown by the great competitors of the car world in the years leading right up to the 1950s: all the champions were middle-aged men with experience as their number one asset.

John Cooper's best rides came very late in his career because he knew the ropes. At 21, you don't use your head, but with logical thinking and a cool temperament, determination is more important than just being fiery. If you're fiery, you're in one minute and out the next. At the end of the day being consistent is being successful. To win one race through being fiery and finishing last in the rest is not being professional. The top professionals are the ones who have won through and survived. Phil Read might have trodden on anybody, but people respected him. The same applies to all the successful runners who are 'hard' guys.

Of the two ways of doing business I still believe it's far better to do everything honestly and fairly as opposed to screwing the deal round to your own advantage. If you have something for sale at the right price, it will be bought; if it's overpriced, no-one will buy. As a racer, you're a saleable item and it's important to get the sale price right.

Grant emphasises that he rides purely for personal satisfaction; it's incidental if people come to see him perform. But the magnetism of the sport has made the association one from which he will never split. Away from the race track, he is often found on a motocross or trials bike practising in nearby fields; his business activities revolve around bikes; and one of his hobbies is collecting old British single-cylinder motorcycles.

Yet he gets no pleasure from taking a tuned motorcycle out for day-to-day riding on public roads. He would much rather give his Sunbeam Lion (a 600cc sidevalve collector's item) an outing at 40 mph.

I just love riding motorcycles and it's human nature to get a kick out of something you do well. With motorcycling, the more you do it the better you do it.

People ask me what feelings I get from going fast. If I took my bike up to 180 mph, it would excite me to a degree, but I wouldn't reach the same level of excitement as a non-racer taking the same bike up to 120 mph. We tend to get rather blasé about speed, but I can assure anyone that we can still see at 180 mph or we wouldn't be going at that pace.

Curiously enough, high-speed lap records leave few lasting impressions. The significance

of becoming the fastest motorcyclist in the United Kingdom, when he smashed the lap record at the 1975 North-West 200 meeting on the Northern Ireland road circuit, meant more to Grant's fans than to him.

In a ten-mile circuit like that, you're actually learning the way as you're racing because there's so little opportunity to practice. On a road circuit – over a much longer distance than the short circuits – it's much easier to knock several seconds off the lap record, as opposed to perhaps a tenth of a second on a short circuit. Whenever your riding is bang on form, it doesn't seem an effort to go very fast. You seem to be touring round while you are actually going exceptionally quickly. Sometimes, when really trying hard, I've had the bike in real slides and I've braked past the limit, but it can be a fabulous feeling to achieve something that captures the public's imagination. That particular day it all clicked and, to be truthful, it came easy.

The Irish papers were full of stories about how an Englishman had conquered the country's fastest circuit with a lap speed of 122·62 mph, seven mph faster than the old record. Grant has always thoroughly enjoyed racing in Ulster because of the nature of the circuits. In return, the crowds have always afforded him a hero's welcome.

In fact, his over-jetted Kawasaki was passed on the fastest section of the first lap by Percy Tait (Yamaha) and Barry Ditch-burn (Kawasaki), but Grant was confident that his experience would put him ahead on the twisty bends of the coast road. His satisfaction in taking the lap record was all the greater for knowing that he did not have the fastest bike in that 1975 race.

Maintaining a relatively high level of fitness is another vital attribute and, with the help of regular trials riding and occasional winter running, Grant remains as sharp as his rivals. Ideal racing weight should be somewhere between eight and 11 stone and height should be between 5ft 5in and 5ft 10in – small enough to be able to ride the tiddler machines yet big enough to be able to hang onto a powerful 750.

Because of his diminutive size, Bill Ivy must have had great difficulty holding onto a 750 Yamaha, whereas Mike Hailwood might have been too big for a 50cc machine. Chop four inches off the legs of Gregg Hansford and the giant would be as successful as Kork Ballington on the small bikes.

Even if a rider is outside the perfect dimensions, however, physical and mental fitness can make up for the shortcomings. Be physically fit and I believe you're halfway to being mentally fit. You don't find any top-line racer these days going out to sink seven or eight pints each night. Competition is so keen now you wouldn't get away with it. I can remember times when Sheene and I came back into the paddock at Scarborough at four in the morning, quite

opposite
Grant takes to the air over Ballaugh Bridge on his way to victory in the 1978 TT Classic

below
Prior to the appearance of the John Player Norton, the three-cylinder BSA Rocket was the last world-beating British motorcycle. In the hands of John Cooper, it beat the best in racing, including Agostini on his all-conquering MV Agusta

well oiled, yet still won the following day. Couldn't do it now, though.

Before the big Formula 750 TT in 1973, Grant acted like the professional he is, retiring to bed at his Douglas boarding house early in the evening. His mechanic Paul Dallas, however, preferred to sample the Douglas night-life – always in plentiful supply during TT fortnight – and was advised to take a door key with him to save disturbing anyone upon his return.

A hot, muggy Isle of Man night and the constant roar of traffic stopped Grant from drifting off to sleep. At about one in the morning, he heard his name being called out from the street, his mind registering in a flash that it was his spannerman wanting to be let in after forgetting his key.

I was really angry. I wasn't going to let him in because I felt he should have had more consideration for other people. Then a stone came through the open window and landed on my stomach. Still I refused to get up. A few seconds later, I could see a silhouette at the window and he must have shinned two floors up the drain pipe. I was livid by then and he got the message that, if he didn't get down before I got to him, I'd kill him. But after lying there for ten minutes, I felt sorry for him, so I went downstairs absolutely stark naked and opened the

Barry Sheene, known world-wide for his exploits both on and off the track

66

front door, expecting to find Paul waiting to come in. My timing was disastrous. As I opened the door, a policeman was looking straight at me. All I could think of to say to him as I stood there without a stitch on was: 'There's a young chap outside, have you seen anything of him.' The policeman gave me such a queer look that I slammed the door and bolted back upstairs. As it happened, Paul had gone off to stay the night with a mechanic friend.

To gain greater public identity, riders at the top persevere with one number in order to be more easily recognised. While Sheene is readily associated with 7, Grant has tried to make 10 his own, although the FIM decrees that riders must assume a number in grands prix which corresponds with their place in the previous year's points table.

It's not done on superstitious grounds. If people cannot recall my name or my bike, they will most likely be able to remember my number.

Many riders do, however, place great store in superstition – especially Sheene – but Grant threw off the last vestige of it during an incident at Silverstone. His grandmother had instilled in him the perils of picking up a glove he might accidentally drop and he believed bad luck would dog him if he did not ask someone else to pick up the glove . . . until

just before his Silverstone ride, there was no-one around but him to gather his fallen glove. He thought he might crash but, after winning the race, he ignored superstition for good.

But whatever the on-track problems and dangers, Grant considers riding the motorbike to be the easy part.

The real struggle is to get the bikes, the backing, the recognition and the publicity. Come the day of the race and the bike is lined up ready to roll, that's what you've toiled for. You're not doing it for the ego bit that might bring you ten minutes of television coverage or an invitation to a club dinner as guest of honour. No, the easy bit is the riding, and it's the bit you enjoy most.

Often nervous as an after-dinner speaker, Grant recognises the publicity value of such exercises but knows that his forte is racing a motorcycle. Compiling notes for a speech is something he finds harder than preparing for a crucial race.

It all depends on what you want to do. I used to work 16 hours a day in my workshop before I could afford a mechanic and it seemed like 16 minutes, because I found it enjoyable.

Before his fatal crash while practising for the East German GP on an MZ, Bill Ivy ranked as one of the top racers in the world on 125cc and 250cc Yamahas

BEGINNINGS

*I'm convinced you're not born with ability, just
the desire to pursue something with all the
enthusiasm you can muster.*

Born the only son of a coal-face worker in
the small mining community of Middlestown,
a few miles from Wakefield in West Yorkshire, Mick Grant and his younger sister
Cheryl grew up amid an atmosphere of ter-
raced housing, allotments and pit-head
friendliness.

Father 'Sammy', a well-known local character from whom Grant derives his lively
sense of humour, was said to have stopped
voting Labour when his son bought a
Mercedes!

As with most aspiring young racers who
made it to the top, Grant had a particular
fascination with anything mechanical from
an early age.

While other kids played football, Grant
would sit on a redundant 250cc JAP roadster
which his father had bought for £60 and subsequently found too fast for his liking.

*Why I should have wanted to play with this
old motorbike, I never have worked out. There
was no interest in the family, I hardly ever
listened to any of the race reports on the radio
and we didn't have any of the motorcycle
magazines in the house.*

His interest progressed to push-bikes, doc-
tored for rough riding through the nearby
woods; later, he began tinkering with friends'
old motorcycles. Most weekends, he was
away youth-hostelling around the north of
England, often seeking the solitude of the
Dales.

After being introduced to the sport as a
teenage spectator, he began riding motorcycles on the road from his 16th birthday,
using his father's 125cc BSA Bantam –
'30 mph in second gear if really pushed.'

*The first road race meeting I saw was at
Scarborough, which is probably why the place
has a great fascination for me.*

Watching the aces of the 1950s, such as
Mike Hailwood, Alistair King and Bob
McIntyre gave him a feeling for the sport
that was to become an obsession.

The same friend whose father had first
introduced him to motorcycling obtained a
350cc Triumph Tiger 80 for the two school
chums to play with in the fields. The petrol
coupons (it was the time of the Suez crisis)
that went with the bike also came in very

handy for the father's car!

A string of extremely cheap motorcycles to
scramble through the woods as a diversion
from his studies at grammar school and college maintained the association.

As a schoolboy, young Grant was considered a late starter. An eleven-plus exam
failure, he made a late jump from Secondary
Modern to Grammar school through his aptitude for fine art, which later earned him a
place at Batley Art College.

His painting and drawing ability marked
him down as a future art teacher but his heart
was a million miles away from his studies. He
lacked the enthusiasm to successfully apply
himself although his art tutor claimed Grant
had more talent in his little finger than he –
the teacher – possessed in his whole body.

*I wasted a lot of years at college. I just didn't
know what I wanted to do in life and spent many
hours worrying about my future.*

The nearest thing to racing in the Grant
family blood was his father's interest in grey-
hounds. But young Grant soon knew the
excitement of two wheels: when his father
would go to bed after returning from night
shift at the colliery, Grant would whip out
the baffles from the Bantam's silencers, hare
down to the woods, and then restore the
machine to its former cleanliness when he
returned.

When he reached the legal age to drive, he
acquired a 2T Villiers Panther, made in neigh-
bouring Cleckheaton, and a 250cc AJS
Sapphire, which suffered frequent big end
failures.

He could not have been called a sports-
lover, although he did enjoy such pursuits as
potholing and climbing. He was still aim-
lessly wandering through life, unsure of his
future and undecided over which career to
choose.

Turning his back on a chance to teach, he
left college at 19 and took a job doing clerical
and photographic work in a local hospital.
His parents gave him an early 21st birthday
cash present of which he invested £140 in the
500cc Velocette that was to start his racing
career.

*After a couple of years at art college I real-
ised it wasn't for me, although the grounding in
art has still left me with an appreciation of
pictures. The training hasn't done me any harm,
but I feel I'm more of a manual worker with*

grubby fingernails than an artist with a brush and palette. Maybe it's because my background is very much working class.

Life was all so aimless for me then, so I thought: 'Stuff it'. I had a Velocette Venom on the road and decided I wanted to go racing. At the time I couldn't make up my mind between road racing or scrambling – but it had to be speed events.

To go scrambling, he would have to buy a proper machine costing several hundred pounds, but his 500cc Velocette could be stripped down and would be competitive enough for club-level racing.

There was still very little ambition inside me. Parents ask toddlers what they want to be when they grow up and the reply from the kids will be a doctor or a nuclear physicist or something. But the gap between reality and ambition is far too big. Rather than standing at the bottom rung of the ladder looking up at the top, I'd much rather take one rung at a time.

Although his parents had toiled to give him a decent education so that he could escape the usual pattern of life – most local school leavers immediately became miners – Grant's father never stood in his way when he chose to take up racing in preference to a steady job.

He never pushed me like you see happening today to some kids, whose fathers never had the opportunity as lads but who now want to enjoy having their sons as successful schoolboy scramblers and grass trackers. I think that's sad in a way.

So he had the backing – if not financially – of his father, but mother Dora was firmly against her son racing motorcycles.

Every year, she asks me if this will be my final season. If she comes to a meeting, she'd sooner sit in the car than watch me race.

Grant taught himself to weld and how to work a lathe and was soon capable of doing his own servicing, which he fitted in between his variety of jobs.

I'd tried the education bit – and failed – so I was then determined to do what I wanted to do. I went looking for the highest-paid job I could find, regardless of what the actual work was, merely to earn enough to go racing.

Grant signed on as an unskilled labourer in a local steel mill. He did 12-hour stints, working nights every alternate week, doing what to him seemed boring and strenuous work. Only the fat pay packet stopped him from quitting.

It makes me laugh now when people say I have had it easy. On the face of it, I suppose they're right, but I reckon I've had to work bloody hard to get where I am.

Like many of the tough Yorkshiremen around him, he found the work sapped the body of almost all strength. Relief would come in the half-hour lunch break, but even then Grant would dart into the fitter's shop

to practice aluminium welding. In unofficial breaks, he would take oxy-acetylene gear into nearby disused kilns to make spares for the Velocette.

Because I needed a full eight hours' sleep, working a night shift left me two hours each day to get the bike prepared for the next meeting. Working at the mill I used to deploy time and motion techniques in my mind to ensure that those two hours were utilised to maximum efficiency.

The road racing bug had bitten him hard. When the final night shift of the week was over at six in the morning, Grant would take a quick shower at the factory and drive his Morris Minor and the trailer with his machine aboard straight to a circuit.

Like so many first-timers, Grant wanted to sample the sport without emptying his pockets. His Croft debut saw the prized Velocette – minus lamps – sporting a home-made hump-back seat made of wood, polystyrene and imitation leather. With standard road tyres and an open exhaust, his outlay had been minimal.

I wanted to have a gallop round to see if I still fancied racing the following year. I wasn't sure whether I'd be too frightened to carry on.

That morning, the County Durham circuit was swathed in autumnal mist and, when everyone was let out for the first practice session, Grant was petrified to have other bikes going past 50 mph faster than him as he attempted to find his way around the circuit. The first actual race was still practice for Grant, who had yet to find the right lines.

His first success, however, came at scrutineering. To hide a bulge in the wall of his front tyre, he let down the air pressure to 10 pounds – and the scrutineers were none the wiser. When pumped back up to 22 pounds, the bulge appeared again and on right-handers, Grant could hear the tyre rubber catching on the tarmac. Despite this handicap, he came 17th out of 40 starters in his heat and finished half-way down the field in the final.

I must have been feeling the same as any proud beginner. At one bend I thought no-one in racing history could have laid the bike over as much as I was doing. I felt like Hailwood.

His pride took a nose dive when Robin Fitton, an acknowledged short circuit expert, passed on the outside of the bend next time round. Grant couldn't believe that other competitors could travel so quickly.

But it wasn't long before he tasted real satisfaction: two years after that first shot of inflicted humility, riding almost the same bike, although now with racing tyres and efficient brakes, Grant beat Fitton at the same Croft meeting.

This was a classic example of what a bit of experience can do. It proved to me that getting in racing mileage was a far better bet than buying fancy bikes. Experience is the most important thing in the world. If you have good bikes at the start, you haven't the know-how to ride them, so it's best to buy something that you can afford to race every weekend, because dicing is the same whether it's with the first guy or last.

You can go to a race and laugh at the guy who is last, thinking you could do much better. Often, that chap who is last is trying harder than the one who's leading the race. Speed doesn't matter, it's what's going on in your mind that counts. I certainly knew that if I was last in spite of trying hard I would still enjoy it.

I just wanted to take a bike to its limit and be in control of it when it was on that fine edge. Suddenly, I had found something I wanted to do more than anything else in the world. Whether or not I would come out on top either financially or physically didn't enter into it.

In those days, Grant, like many a young motorcyclist, was out every night frequenting public houses, before he became serious about the sport.

On a good night, I might have had as many as ten pints. It would be down to the working men's club for a right good sing-song.

But the man with the ferocious red beard, who emerged on race days from a tiny tent to cook baked beans for breakfast over a primus stove, had the determination to persevere seriously with road racing. Socialising was put aside as he sought success on the track.

I never thought of myself as being good enough to make a living out of racing. Really, what I did at the time was suicidal. It would have been safer to have pursued my college course and become a teacher earning a good salary.

Two years as a coiler were followed by a spell as a fork-lift truck driver in a carpet factory, which gave him more free time to prepare his Velocette. Even before his debut in road racing, this machine was taking him to high placings in Yorkshire tarmac hill climbs.

With a standard engine, the Velocette pushed out around 45 bhp. It had a four-speed, close-ratio gearbox with a dry clutch, was housed in a special duplex frame which Grant had modified and it had a home-made single front disc brake. Maximum revs were 6,200 rpm, with the top speed somewhere around 118 mph. Grant has always maintained that it was one of the nicest handling bikes he's ever ridden.

After finding his feet in club events, the Batley Motorcycle Club member's first expedition overseas took him in 1967 to the Carrowdore 100 in the rolling countryside of Northern Ireland.

It was too bold a step at that stage of my career. I frightened myself to death. But I'd heard other lads speak of the good times they'd had over in Northern Ireland, so I thought I

would have a bit of a dabble.

After towing the bike to Heysham with his ageing Morris, Grant wheeled the Velocette aboard the ferry, together with a box of spanners. At Belfast docks, the collection of racing machines were transported by lorry to Bally-walter, near the circuit, while the riders, Grant amongst them, enjoyed the comparative luxury of bed and breakfast in a church hall. Next day, as he rode his untaxed and uninsured racer to the circuit, he was stopped by a police patrol car whose occupants warned him, not about his law-breaking, but about the rules forbidding any practise on the Carrowdore circuit before the roads were closed.

Since the five-mile natural circuit was completely unknown to him and there was to be no practising or even the benefit of a warm-up lap, he took up the offer of a local to show him the way round on his scooter. After insisting that they should enjoy a couple of glasses of Guinness before they set off, this Ulsterman then proceeded to head in the opposite direction to the circuit. He was, in fact, going to the old course which had been shortened that year. As precious time slipped by, some advice from Grant had the scooter heading back to the paddock, where he quickly accepted the offer of a one-lap ride on a 150cc Triumph

Terrier which had a rattling big end.

It was as narrow as Oliver's Mount, twice as bumpy and with piles of cow-pats all over the road. Luckily, in the race, the slip-ring in the magneto slipped and the bike stopped. I've never been as thankful in my life before. It scared me to death – so much so that I went back the following year!

His next visit saw him familiarising himself with the course in the chair of a friend's sidecar. During the newly permitted warm-up lap, Grant lost the seat of his Velo. A minute after the pack of 60 charged off, he just managed to secure the saddle. By lap three, he was in the thick of the action.

Looking back, I really shudder. I was riding recklessly, to say the least. I took four of them at one bend with the bike in the gutter, shot up the slip road in a panic and, as I powered the machine back onto the circuit, it high-sided me and I was off. The footrest had come off and the seat had worked loose again, so I had to call it a day.

To me that's what real road racing is all about and it's just ridiculous to suggest that modern bikes are too fast for these circuits. If you can ride a motorbike, you should be able to race everywhere. It's all about adapting to the circumstances.

Apart from replacement clutch plates, to-

Grant's first road racing machine, a 500cc Velocette. While youngsters are now encouraged to begin on small capacity bikes, Grant started in the 500cc class because it was the most economical class to contest at the time

71

gether with the occasional set of new tyres, Grant's only real outlay went on entry fees; with luck, he was usually able to recoup that expense from prize money. While other newcomers were splashing out on special components to improve their machines, despite lacking the skill to use the modifications to their full potential, Grant preferred to conserve his money for entry fees and petrol. As his racing lessons began to take effect, Grant experienced one of the harsher realities of life during a 'Stars of Tomorrow' meeting at Mallory Park, where he was knocked out after being thrown from his Velocette while leading. These were days of the pudding-basin helmet, which offered precious little protection to the head. Because he did not want to alarm his parents with reports of head injuries, he discharged himself from a Leicester hospital the same evening and returned to work the next day.

When he experimented with fuel injection during another meeting at Croft, Grant's engine cut out at 90 mph. Trying to rectify the problem as he sped along the main straight, he lost control and ploughed in the barriers, injuring his arm but somehow staying on the machine.

These were good lessons to learn at such an early age, at speeds that couldn't get me into too much bother. Fiddle about with the motor of a 750 while travelling at 130 mph and you'd be through the hedge before you knew it.

By this time, he had become a door-to-door salesman, endeavouring to foist household needs upon unsuspecting housewives. It was the Austin A35 van that went with the job that appealed most to Grant, because it also provided transport for his race machines.

I had to work Saturday mornings because the women still had some money left from their husbands' pay packets of the previous day. One day I had an hour between finishing work and getting to the start of the Esholt sprint near Bradford sewerage works. I just had my boots to put on as I heard the announcer calling my class out for practice, but my granny had packed the inside of my boots tight with small balls of paper to maintain the shape. The paper was almost impossible to get out. By the time I had scratched out the last ball, I'd missed first practice by half an hour.

As his interest in racing became all-consuming, the nights of mild and bitter with the boys were left behind, but there was nothing yet to suggest he was a star in the making.

Such was his passion, however, that he was willing to trade in his job as a fork-lift truck driver for a fortnight's competition in the Manx GP.

The boss couldn't comprehend how someone would want to sacrifice a good job for a bit of sport. People like that are on completely different wavelengths.

His Manx debut (in 1969) saw him finish last in the Senior race, which was not as bad as it would appear. The Velocette stopped on the descent from Hilberry on the third lap because the contact breaker gap had closed on his home-made coil ignition system and Grant manfully pushed it all the way to the pits so that the problem could be diagnosed. The 20-minute delay had cost him a lap and any hope of claiming the newcomer's award.

Funnily enough, the TT never frightens me these days, because everything is under control. But that first time, I was in a panic on every corner and it's easy to see how people who are inexperienced at that type of riding can get into bother. But I just had to race in the Island. I've considered myself a pure motorcyclist and the TT is real road racing. I used to read about the races in books and I would sneak out of college to listen to the radio commentaries on Phil Read battling against Bill Ivy. There was a magical ring to the place and I felt I had to go and ride around it.

As has been the case throughout his racing career, Grant prepared himself thoroughly. He went over to the Isle of Man the weekend preceding the racing to discover which way the circuit went and spent the first night with his girlfriend in a sleeping bag under a hedge near Union Mills.

The second night was like being in seventh heaven – we slept on the pebbles on Ramsey beach!

Knowing that he would have to spend £70 to cover his racing, he tried to conserve money in every way. During race week, he camped in a tent in the paddock – unaware that in six years' time he would be the TT lap record holder and a resident at the Island's top hotel.

We went round on a bus trip on which one of the leading riders gave us a corner-by-corner description. Well, 90 per cent was quickly forgotten but the ten per cent I remembered were the instructions for Parliament Square in Ramsey. On my first lap, doing as the man said, my not hitting the wall at May Hill must have been an act of God. My friend, Peter Laverack, went five miles an hour quicker on the same line and hit the wall, seriously hurting himself. I've learned that whatever someone tells you, never take it as fact. A lot of people say they do Bray Hill in top gear and they actually believe they do it that way. But watch them and you'll see they're few and far between. It's so easy to be misled. The only way to find out is to do it yourself.

As he began to secure reasonable placings on his road-going Velocette – competing against proper racing tackle – Grant attracted the attention of the Birstall frame-maker Jim Lee, who offered sponsorship.

An experimental Lee frame made the Velo a competitive machine and, when Grant went to work for the firm as a welder, the plan was

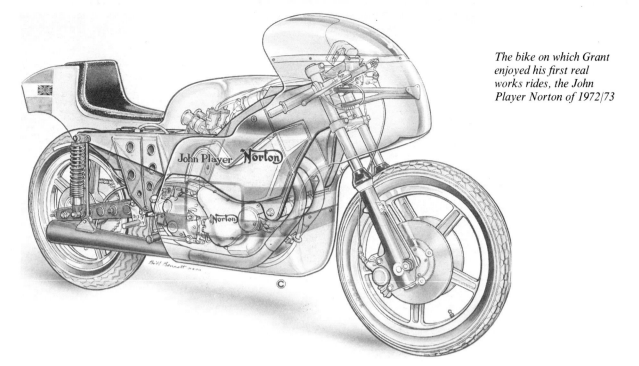

to obtain a Norton Commando engine and house it in a special frame. The Commando was then in the public eye because of track successes by fellow Yorkshireman Tony Jefferies.

As it was almost impossible to lay hands on a Norton motor, however, Grant and Lee settled for a BSA Gold Star power unit as a stop-gap measure.

If there was an early milestone in Grant's successful career, perhaps it was at Cadwell in 1971, when he beat Charlie Sanby – much-respected at that time – on his Norton Commando, to record his first National class win. The prize just covered the bill for tuning and Grant was to long cherish the look on the face of his backer. The decals on Grant's helmets throughout his racing bore the man's initials – JL – in recognition of his assistance.

The short spell with the single-cylinder BSA Gold Star, although relatively successful, was costly. As it revved faster than the heavier Velocette, broken pistons and big ends had to be replaced every six meetings. The next machine was Jim Lee's 350cc Yamaha TR2, an air-cooled twin-cylinder machine with a wet clutch and six-speed gearbox. The spine frame was made of 3-inch diameter steel tubing. Although fitted with Seeley forks, the green-and-orange bike did not handle as well as anticipated and Grant found that the bike would not fire up first time on starting a race with the plugs hot; the only way to ensure a good start was to replace them on the grid with dry plugs.

Grant went on to win 16 successive races at club and national level on the Yamaha and even managed to win a silver replica in his first Isle of Man TT after only that one previous visit to the Manx GP.

If any man has been synonymous with TT racing in the 1970s, that man is Grant. Every

year his name is the one guaranteed to get thousands of fans talking and he has rarely let them down, although some of his Island performances were less auspicious than others. In the 1971 750cc race, riding his Commando on what should have been a 102 mph opening lap, he fetched another rider off at Signpost corner.

I had him in my sights at Cronk-ny-Mona and knew I had to pass him before Signpost or I would have been held up all the way to Governor's Dip. But I went sailing under him about 30 mph too fast, brought him off and laid him out.

By this time, Grant (and sponsor Jim Lee) had recognised the publicity value of racing in colours that stood out – like apple green leathers and a candy-apple metallic green fairing with orange exhaust pipes, but his Norton Commando still had only a standard engine with four gears.

But that standard engine, with just a bit of

breathing-on, was a very competitive motor and was the thing to win with in 1971. It just shows how quickly development takes place: six years later that bike would have been lapped after three laps.

With such a wide torque band, the four-speed gearbox was quite adequate. The duplex frame, produced by Grant and Lee, had no bottom rungs and the engine was suspended by four rubber bobbins. It revved to 7,000 rpm with power from 4,000 rpm. The Commando sported a single front disc brake and a Manx Norton rear wheel. Various electronic ignition units were tried, but Grant eventually reverted to the proven, if old-fashioned, coil ignition.

The major problem with the engine at that time (and, later, with the John Player Norton) was that the bottom end was not strong enough for the power, so that the crankcase would break.

Pre-race nerves often make Grant pay a visit to the toilet just before he takes his place on the grid, but before the 1971 Junior TT, he was unable to produce much in the gent's prior to the five-lap event.

I set off confident that it would be one department I wouldn't have to worry about. But by Quarter Bridge on the opening lap, I was suddenly bursting to go. It was incredible. My plan was to stop at the pits next time round which would only cost me a couple of minutes but, as I rounded the Gooseneck, I was given a sign to

The pull of the open roads – Grant in his element on his 352cc Yamaha in the 1973 Senior TT

say Agostini, the red-hot favourite, was out. This meant that the top-liners – Chatterton, Jefferies, Rutter and company – would all be trying harder for the first prize, which might lead to a lot of bike breakages and that would shoot me up the order. As the last thing to do was to waste time, I pressed on, still in a lot of discomfort. I was so desperate to go that I couldn't concentrate on my lines, so I decided to find a corner where there were no spectators and stop there next time round. But around all those 38 miles, there were people everywhere, so that idea was out. There was only one thing left to do – pee inside my leathers. Then I thought about how I would look if the bike broke down at an out-of-the-way place like Windy Corner. I'd be caught steaming and smelling really anti-social, stuck there as an outcast for three hours because the sidecar race was next. With my position improving all the time, I decided that if the bike made four laps I would risk messing the leathers on the final circuit.

After crossing the line for the fourth time, I stood on the pegs, cocked one leg over one side, then did the same with the other, but I just couldn't make anything happen. It was agony all the way round. As I got the chequered flag to take seventh place, I roared up the green lane in third gear with the wheel spinning while the others wearily pushed their bikes in with folks patting them on the back. I just missed a guy in a white smock who wanted the bike stuck in the finisher's enclosure, parked against the gent's and had the most satisfying two minutes I've ever had in the Isle of Man.

Grant now settles himself mentally for a race and, although a repeat of the experience is something he dreads every time in the Island, cramp is more likely to pose a problem. He guards against this with glucose drinks and salt tablets.

Grant now appeared to be leaving his contemporaries at club level behind and events were taking a turn for the better that would help him advance in what was to become his profession.

Following discussions with Lee, the pair decided that it would be in Grant's interest to move a few miles down the road to Padgetts of Batley – a large, thriving motorcycle concern who would be able to provide machines and a job in the workshop. These were over-the-counter factory Yamahas which required only normal maintenance. Grant now had the opportunity to race the new 350 TR2 Yamaha, the first air-cooled Japanese twin with a dry clutch and which Grant found to be a superb machine.

The reason for leaving Jim Lee was that I needed the race-proven machines which Padgetts could supply. I was now on the same machines as everyone else and I had a yard-stick to see if I had the ability to make a go of it.

The six-speed Yamaha had drum brakes back and front and the suggested power output was something in the region of 60 bhp with a top speed of 145 mph. It revved to 10,500 rpm with the power coming in at 7,000 rpm.

It was absolutely reliable. Of all the races I did on it, the machine never let me down once. You just had to look at the bike and it would start, and good starts on the very latest machinery improved my chances no end.

He also got a bored-out, 354cc bike for 500cc events, but disagreement over financial matters made the association far from amicable. Even though Grant won 30 races on the Padgett machines and was leading both 350cc and 500cc British Championships, he needed no second invitation from team manager Frank Perris to become the third rider in the John Player Norton team, a well-backed set-up that promised to do so much for the dying British bike cause.

But the Padgett deal also gave Grant the opportunity to race a Kawasaki for the first time. Supplied by Agrati, then importers of the marque, he took third place in the 1972 Senior TT on an air-cooled three-cylinder 500 behind the two MV Agustas of Agostini and Pagani. He failed to achieve his first ton-up TT lap by a whisker, having lapped at 99·9 mph. By anyone's standards, that 1972 TT was a good one for Grant, bearing in mind that it takes some time to get to know the full Mountain Circuit.

It's a question of doing your homework and, with the exception of a few places, there isn't a circuit in the world that I haven't walked all the way round. Then you should drive and ride round it – that's the only way to learn.

In the Junior TT that year, Grant led Tony Rutter by 30 seconds, until the clutch nipple came out of the gearbox.

I have never professed to being a brave man and one thing I wouldn't do in the Isle of Man is ride round without a clutch.

He began to 'tour' home through Hilberry when he realised his sister Cheryl had come over to the TT for the first time especially to see big brother in action. He had advised her of a fine viewing spot on the right-hand side of the wall at Cronk-ny-Mona.

Being a working-class lass, it had cost her a fair bit to come over so, rather than disappoint her, I thought I would put on a bit of demo for her. I took the Cronk on full bore, then carried on touring back to the pits. But she had already heard over the loudspeakers that I was touring and she was almost speechless at the speed I was travelling. 'What would you have been like if you had actually been racing?' she wondered in amazement. I never did tell her the truth.

It was also the year when master motorcycle tuner Tom Arter put his weight behind a protest to the organising Auto-Cycle Union

to have the engines of the first dozen machines home measured. It was suspected that some 350cc machines used in the 500cc race lacked the eccentric crank pins needed to make them legal 351 or 352cc motors, the class being open to bikes from 351cc to 500cc.

I was upset that someone like Tom Arter should protest when he used to complain bitterly about having the G50 engine ridden by Peter Williams measured. Even though I failed to complete the race because of a 30 mph prang on the oil at Ramsey, I insisted my bike was measured because I didn't like any insinuation that we had been cheating.

Grant was one hundred per cent confident that the Vernier measuring gauge would register just over 351cc. But the operator's calculation came out at 360cc, a figure completely unheard of. At the time, it was only possible to have 351 or 354cc, depending on whether the engine was stroked or bored. When it was announced that Grant had a 360cc motor, he was inundated with enquiries as to how he was able to achieve that capacity; it turned out to be inaccuracy in the official measurement, which made a mockery of the Arter protest.

Grant finally landed his first works contract in the summer of 1972, but his debut ride on the much-publicised John Player Norton was one to forget. On the back straight of Sweden's Anderstorp circuit, Grant was thrown off the machine at 140 mph during practice for the Formula 750 Championship round. The cast-iron flywheel (apparently not designed to rev at 7,000 rpm) split, and a large piece pierced the aluminium crank-case, went through the fairing, hit the road and split the rear tyre. Although the engine appeared to explode, Grant came off because of the disintegrating rear tyre. As he skidded up the track on his backside, he almost caught the Gus Kuhn Norton in front ridden by Dave Potter as he braked for the corner.

The team's new boy met with further disappointment in another Continental ride at Rungis, a hastily-made circuit around a market place near Orly airport on the outskirts of Paris – Grant clobbered racing's Mr. Big, the many-times world champion Giacomo Agostini.

Fellow team-member Phil Read had offered Grant some advice, telling him the advantages of getting to the front on the first lap. 'Get up the inside and outbrake them,' said Read, 'and if you can't do it in the first lap, forget it.'

Because of bad weather and an engine misfire in practice, Grant had little chance to get the feel of the circuit and, when it came to a series of switchbacks, he failed to remember how many of these artificial mounds there were. He couldn't believe his eyes when he saw Agostini just ahead on the MV.

I thought he was braking early and I planned to nip up the inside of him, keeping my bike flat out over the next hump and then I'd begin to brake on the hump after that. But there was one hump less than I thought. My bike was three feet off the ground and I had 60 yards to get it straightened up. I had no chance, nor did Ago who was on the classic racing line. As he came across me on the correct line, I hit him smack on his number plate and walloped him into the straw bales, with me not far behind. The crowd were leaping about in a high state of excitement and, not knowing too much about Continental racing, I thought they might lynch me. I associated mobs in Paris with the guillotine but, just in case these people were Italians, I felt the best thing to do was to get poor old Ago out. I pulled on a boot sticking out of the bales and he came out all right, ranting and raving, even though his face was still enclosed in his full-face helmet.

The MV was righted and, apart from a broken screen, there seemed nothing else wrong. Off went Ago with Grant not far behind, keen to put some distance between himself and the angry-looking crowd. Grant's Norton managed a few more laps before it expired, but each time he passed that section of the crowd, they were waving wildly. It transpired later that they were all anti-Ago and were cheering the Englishman for ruining the Italian's chances. Ago, meanwhile, only managed a further lap and retired dejectedly with a puncture.

He came over to me brandishing a three-inch nail used for knocking wooden cartons together, claiming it had caused his puncture. He insisted that this nail had come off my Norton in the crash. I don't think Frank Perris was too amused by a suggestion that his pride and joy was held together with nails!

Considerably upset at the time, Grant was given a verbal roasting by manager Perris for bringing down Agostini. It was bad for John Player Norton's image, and he could not understand how one works rider could knock another off.

From that day to this, I've always believed that people can make mistakes and it's bloody annoying to knock people off, or to be knocked off, as has happened to me. But it's part of the game and has to be accepted.

Grant's elevation to works team status put him, financially at least, on an even keel, although by today's standards, his JP Norton retainer fee was small. But it was enough to buy him a brace of Yamahas to run privately.

I have never regretted any of my decisions and there were certainly no misgivings about signing for Norton, even though they did eventually sack me. You're better off riding for the lousiest factory team in the world than you are racing as a privateer – that's what I believed at the time. Getting recognition is vital and the

way to do it, apart from winning races, is to be with an outfit that gets publicity, as John Player Norton certainly did at the time.

Unfortunately, the team was a white elephant. The bikes just weren't competitive, despite being super to ride. If they didn't suffer from a misfire due to fuel pump problems, the gearbox would break because there was more horsepower than it had been designed to take. But everything felt perfect when sitting on the bike. It can be very difficult to get mechanics to set up a bike to make it feel nice, but on the Norton, the clutch would operate like silk; you'd never have to tell a Norton mechanic to oil a cable or to make sure it had no kinks in it. The throttle was beautifully light and it would always have new Amal rubber grips on. You wouldn't need great big handfuls to work the brake either. Everything was absolutely perfect. You were, in theory, half-way to winning the race before you even started. Without the gearbox and fuel starvation problems, it would have been a lot, lot more successful.

When Grant first rode the John Player Norton, he felt that it was not quite as quick as the private Commando he had campaigned earlier in his career. The works machinery was heavier with a full fairing and a bigger seat.

I always thought it was incredible for folks to lend me bikes to go racing with, but for them to pay me too, as John Player Norton did, was beyond my wildest dreams.

The fact that the bike did not perform during the half season in which he was contracted to ride it did not leave Grant unimpressed. He only had two wins on it – at Scarborough – but the memory of such an immaculately-prepared machine will always be with him.

The opposition, of course, was stiff with the three-cylinder Triumphs and BSAs as well as the Kuhn Norton being a match for speed, but the longer the team went without the results coming in, the more they became something of a joke.

Because there were often not enough machines to go round all three works riders, Grant would be the man to step down. He didn't mind, because he could then race his own 350 Yamaha which he felt was more competitive anyway.

In fact, Grant had one more ride on a factory Norton the following year, when he made a guest appearance at Scarborough. Grant realised it would put him in a position to get improved start money but Perris instructed him to finish second in the race to his number one rider Peter Williams. Grant sat in second place until Williams came off and went on to win the main prize for the second successive year.

When he discovered that Norton were dispensing with his services, he was dismayed.

I was disappointed when Norton said they

didn't want me. I felt it all boiled down to money. They were possibly keener to pay what Dave Croxford was asking than the sum I wanted.

But when the new Norton engine did not materialise and the team failed to become any more successful, Grant knew he had made the right move, especially as he was enjoying a cracking 1973 season on his Yamahas.

He now had the necessary foundations on which to build a successful career as a privateer on Yamahas, something for which he had much to thank one-time Superbike ace John Cooper.

Grant had got to know Cooper through his first sponsor, Jim Lee. Out of the blue, Cooper offered Grant a pair of new 250 and 350 TZ Yamahas, complete with spares, for no other reason than that he fancied the Yorkshireman would ride them to their full potential. But Grant, with only £300 in the bank and brought up to believe nothing should be purchased on borrowed money, hesitated at the offer. Excited at the chance of being able to be independent and knowing

he was due a lump sum from his Norton contract, he nevertheless kept tossing the deal over in his mind.

Grant finally chose to take the machines and was amazed to hear Cooper say: 'Pay me when you can. I've got faith in you that you'll win the money.' His confidence in that June of 1972 was rewarded less than six months later, when Grant had won enough to pay off the debt. The Yahamas were always in the results, rarely broke down and cost very little to maintain.

He wasn't sponsoring me; he had actually given me the bikes. Half the incentive that year was to repay not just the money, but also the faith he had put in me.

There was nothing to match the Yamaha racing product that could be bought by anyone with enough money, according to Grant. It would go half a season without having a spanner laid on it. With a three-litre Ford Transit van, two bikes of his own and the ability to become Britain's top privateer, Grant now found no difficulty in becoming a full-time professional.

The last great British racing bikes? Grant ahead of his John Player Norton team-mates, Peter Williams and Phil Read, at Scarborough's Oliver's Mount circuit.

FIRST GRANDS PRIX

One-time northern Bultaco ace Brian Richards continually harangued business associate Brian Davidson to supply him with a new racing motorcycle. When Davidson finally agreed, Richards felt he was too old to do justice to a new machine and they decided to search for a promising lad to sponsor: their selection was Mick Grant. Incredibly, Davidson (a self-made millionaire from Gretna Green) had never been to a race meeting in his life, but his interest was to flourish.

With competitive machinery and a sound backer behind him Grant knew the right course of action to take in 1973 was to branch out and make a name for himself. This he did in a big way by racing successfully in South Africa, America and in selected European grands prix. The South African organisers paid him expenses, but Daytona cost him money, even though he was the first British privateer home, in eighth place. Daytona, however, was then a far more significant meeting than it is now.

A super-fast bowl of speed set on Florida's famous coast, Daytona is traditionally the first major meeting on the world calendar and the much-publicised event once attracted riders, works teams, press and spectators from all over the world. It also saw the debut of the year's new machines, which added to the interest. At that time, the ultra-high speeds obtained on the angled banking were beginning to out-pace tyre development, which later led to restrictions on the race to hold down the ever-increasing speeds.

It was here that Grant unpacked the 350cc water-cooled TZ Yamaha from its crate for the beginning of the 1973 season. He had a nerve-racking debut in the 200-miler, feeling insecure with an almost non-existent front drum brake and an ill-handling rear tyre.

One way to get a works bike is to contact the factory personally and simply ask if machinery is available. This is just what Grant did with Ducati, after being very impressed by the speed of their vee-twin model during his stay in Africa. After telexing their Bologna headquarters in Italy to see if he could ride one in the opening European classic at Imola, he was invited to test Ducati's 750cc machine. In the two 100-mile legs of the actual race, he burnt out the clutch at the start of one and was seventh in the other, but the effort was justified by the amount of publicity and for the experience of dealing with Italian factory officials.

They said the machine shouldn't be revved above 10,400 but considering this was supposed to be a lazy old vee-twin, that's some revs. The Kawasaki I rode for several years was a thousand revs short of that figure at the top. We practised on a 500 vee-twin to get the feel of the bike and, incredibly, were told not to go beyond 12,000 rpm on this super short-stroke engine.

On his first visit, Grant was gingerly finding his way round the Modena test track for the first time on the previous year's Ducati, following the factory's number one racer at the time, Bruno Spaggiari, who was riding the new, faster model. The Italian had agreed to show him the way round but seemed to be travelling slower than Grant thought necessary. So Grant went ahead and began to circulate faster with each lap, with Spaggiari hanging on behind him.

To my embarrassment and humiliation I slid off on a bend right in front of all the top Ducati officials. I felt six inches tall while Spaggiari was beaming from ear to ear.

At the end of another day, Spaggiari found himself with a slower lap time than Grant. As soon as he was told of the faster time, Spaggiari gave Grant a big scowl, changed back into his leathers and stayed out until he topped it.

On principle, Grant will never do a full grand prix season without being paid by a factory. The system he used during his first year of GP racing is one he would always adopt if he was without works machinery.

I chose the meetings I wanted to do, perhaps only about 50 per cent of the whole championship programme, because they provided good experience which would help if a work contract did emerge in the future.

His first ever GP hammered home just what that type of racing was all about. He came a battle-weary tenth after riding harder than ever before and he was amazed not to succeed as he would have done in any British national meeting.

There were people I'd lap in England coming past me with ten miles an hour to spare. Yet it wasn't only that. The technique was completely different and left me like a babe-in-arms. At Hockenheim, on the big, horse-shoe bend, I'd be scraping the deck with my foot-rests and

exhausts, getting into broad-sides, then some-one like John Dodds – who was excellent at the time – would come right round me. I just couldn't understand how people like him, using the same tyres as me, could get round a corner more quickly and be in more control than I could.

A quick word with Phil Read led to Grant following the world champion elect in one of the training sessions.

He was actually changing up going into the horse-shoe bend, where I had been on the brakes for 30 yards.

So shattered and demoralised was he after this grand prix baptism that he needed much persuasion to drive south for the next world championship round at Monza, the Italian track's last major motorcycle meeting as it turned out.

Obviously I hadn't gone to my first grand prix thinking I'd win, but I'd hoped to finish in the first five. After working bloody hard to get even tenth, I knew it was a completely different ball-game – and they wouldn't let me play. The whole business so disorientated me, I forgot to pick up my £10 prize money!

Harmony in any racing team is a vital consideration. With long hours spent in each other's company, rider, mechanics, wives and girlfriends all have to be compatible.

Grant had a problem with his wife-to-be Carol and mechanic Paul Dallas during his initial GP sortie abroad. The pair would occasionally squabble and Grant eventually had to decide which one should go.

Paul was a good mechanic, so it had to be Carol. But, to be fair, I adopted the wrestling system, where the miscreant has two public warnings. Well, it didn't take long before the two were arguing over something for a second time, so we put her on the next plane home.

These were days of rough and ready living: the Transit van was the eating and sleeping quarters and most meals were egg and beans cooked on a Primus stove – a long way from the sophisticated five-star hotels and Cordon Bleu cookery which Grant would enjoy when he became an established star.

Grant's second taste of grand prix life was also to stay clearly in his memory, not through any outstanding individual performance, but because he came unscathed through one of racing's blackest days.

Motorcycle racing fans throughout the world were shocked when they heard that the Finn Jarno Saarinen – tipped as one of the future all-time greats – and the popular Italian Renzo Pasolini had lost their lives in a multi-bike pile-up during the 250cc race at that Italian world championship meeting. Some blamed the frightening crash on oil dropped in a previous race, others say that

Grant raced this standard road-going Kawasaki 1,000cc Z1 in Australia's Castrol six-hour race during 1973

79

the engine of Pasolini's Harley-Davidson
seized. Whatever the cause, Grant will never
forget the race. He was back on the third row
of the grid when the starter's flag dropped.

*I have always been able to start a motorbike
quite quickly and a lot of my early success in
England was due to that fact. It was really unheard of for me not to be able to start my
Yamaha. This time I bump-started, then immediately stalled it, which I couldn't believe.
By the time I bumped it again, the first part of
the pack had gone. Normally from my position
on the grid, I'd have been up to the front straight
away; had I been up at the front, I'd have been
right in the thick of that terrible accident.*

Grant was in about 14th place as Grand
Curve approached. The right-hander was
guarded on its left side by a formidable wall

of Armco, the enemy of hundreds of motorcycle racers over the years. On a 250 machine,
it could be taken flat-out. Just. On a quicker
350, a change-down would be needed. The ·
Armco was so close to the track, however,
that any fallen rider would be thrown back
onto the track. On this occasion, apparently,
a couple of the leading riders took the bend
comfortably, then Pasolini's bike seized, re-
bounded off the barrier and took down
Saarinen. For the next ten seconds, there was
bedlam.

*Everything was happening – bikes in the air,
fires, smoke. It was the most horrible experience of my life. I remember Bo Jansson falling
off in front of me and I was trying to miss him.
I was braking hard but I couldn't see a way
through the mass of bikes, petrol tanks and*

bodies. *I would have been doing 120 mph and there was just nowhere to go. There were people crashing behind me and a petrol tank came over my head as I applied the brakes. My intention was to get off the bike somehow before I hit something hard, but for some reason I changed my mind and decided to stay on. Miraculously, a way through emerged and I was clear. I felt so relieved that I just carried on for a further lap and came back round to the crash, where I did my best to help Chas Mortimer, who had injured his knee-cap. I can remember him saying at the time that both Saarinen and Pasolini were dead.*

While the organisers abandoned the meeting, Grant was sitting in a trance back in the paddock, intensely shocked by the whole sorry affair.

Saarinen would have been one of the greats. It was such a shame, especially as the accident was none of his making. He was a real engineer who was in complete control of the preparation of his bikes. You could often walk back to your van at any time of the night and Saarinen would be working on his engine: he had an enormous appetite for work. Jarno Saarinen helped bring me on no end when he came to Britain. I know he had the ability and the tackle to play around with me, which he did, but he drew me ahead of the top home runners.

Amazingly, Grant managed to escape through the Monza carnage without mishap. He keeps a yellowing newspaper cutting at home showing him as the solitary rider appearing through the smoke from the track 'battlefield', a reminder of the afternoon that will always live in his mind.

While the Yamaha of 1972 was a great success, the same could not be said of the following year's model, which switched to water-cooling – a system that allowed a greater control of the engine temperature, but which also produced a bike that persisted in breaking bearings. The 1974 standard Yamaha went a little quicker and was more reliable but tyre technology, then in its infancy, could not quite match the power output.

Ripples of excitement were being caused by a growing trend towards lightweight two-stroke 750 bikes with the lively, one-wheeling Suzukis in the hands of the Americans delighting home crowds. The heavier British three-cylinder bikes were on their way out.

Three other grand prix rides that year, including a useful fourth in the Dutch TT, made Grant realise he was shaping up, although a lot of attention would have to be paid to the preparation of the machines.

Back at home, I wouldn't need to look at a carburettor main jet or a sparking plug. Top speed in England didn't matter. At Brands Hatch, for instance, if one bike is 20 mph quicker than another, the slower one can equalise the speed differential by being ridden harder. But with grands prix and their very long straights, two mph difference is a make-or-break gap. And some of the other bikes were up to 10 mph faster. In England, even if the jet was six sizes out, the thing would still run and you'd be OK. On the Continent, they had carburation settings down to a fine art and piston clearances were spot-on, to get the absolute maximum out of the engine.

Three great stars who thrilled thousands throughout Europe – Tepi Lansivuori (left), Giacomo Agostini (centre) and Phil Read.

THE KAWASAKI YEARS

Those who succeed at the highest level of racing have many treasured moments to look back on. Grant's most memorable ride came in the 1977 Dutch TT at Assen, in front of 150,000 spectators, when he gave the new 250cc Kawasaki in-line twin its first grand prix win. It was his first proper GP outing on the bike, Kawasaki's programme of world championship racing placing team-mate Barry Ditchburn in the saddle for the first half of the grand prix season, while Grant assumed responsibility for the rest of the campaign.

While this was done because of a meagre racing budget (and because Kawasaki wanted to stay in the hunt for the Superbike Championship in Britain), Grant was dismayed to be given his chance on the new bike so late; but he was the one who insisted that the machine was a potential winner once its vibration problem had been cured. As he was the last to ride the machine – after Ditchburn, Frenchman Jean-Françoise Balde and the

Japanese factory riders, Akihiro Kiyohara and Masahiro Wada – Grant felt there was a team bias against him.

The plan was for Grant to do the grand prix immediately after the Isle of Man TT, but the next round was in Yugoslavia and Motor Circuit Developments would only release one Kawasaki rider from their Mallory Post-TT meeting contract. Ditchburn therefore carried on in the classics, as he already had some points to his name from earlier rounds. The situation left Grant unhappy and frustrated and a certain amount of acrimony – unseen by the public – existed between the rider and other members of the team.

When I was prevented from racing in Yugoslavia – which had been agreed would be my first – I was, to say the least, disappointed. It may seem immodest of me to say now that I could have won the world championship that year with a full season's racing, but the results once I started showed that I would have had a good chance of doing so.

With its workings laid bare, the mighty Kawasaki which Grant rode with such success until his switch to Honda at the end of 1978

Aboard the big Kawasaki

When Grant was finally sent to Holland to attack the grands prix he promised John Norman, racing chief of Kawasaki UK, that he would win the race.

From time to time a feeling comes over me that I can win a certain race and I felt certain that I would do well at the Dutch. But I had so little experience on the bike that I wondered if I was being over-optimistic. There was I, in at the deep end, competing against blokes who had been riding 250s all season.

By the end of the third practice session, Grant was third fastest and separated from the first two – Alan North and Ditchburn – by less than a second. But before the race there was more aggravation. When a Kawasaki director sounded surprised by Grant's quick time, Grant felt that misleading information about his ability was being relayed to the factory personnel.

I was so angry that night I didn't sleep at all. When I did set off in the race, I pushed so hard on the handlebars through intense anger that I thought I might bend them.

Grant was first away and looked untouchable, increasing his lead lap by lap until he was given the sign 'plus 26 seconds'. With only four laps of the 4·796-mile van Drenthe circuit remaining, and rain beginning to fall, he began to cruise on his slick-shod Kawasaki. But as everyone assumed he was in a safe posi-

tion, the Kawasaki technicians concentrated on giving pit signals only to Ditchburn in an effort to improve his placing. With the board still showing he was 26 seconds up, Grant naturally thought that everyone else in the race was, like him, slowing because of the wet track. It was on the last lap that he was given a rude awakening, with the news that his lead had been slashed to just seven seconds by the Harley-Davidson rider, Franco Uncini.

I thought, 'Christ! That person is going like a rocket and will catch me half way round the last lap.' So I really hammered it, which was a stupid thing to do in the rain. I was sliding all over the place and could have easily tossed it up the road. By increasing the gap to almost 11 seconds, I was able to win with ease, but the build-up before the race made the victory specially satisfying.

Not only was Grant over the moon, but the Japanese technicians were highly delighted as well. They could report the first GP success of that machine and some of them would also be allowed to return home to their families now that the initial breakthrough had been made.

At that particular time, the win was the most important thing that had ever happened to me but I was filled with frustration because there was proof that, barring a disaster, a world title could have been achieved if I'd had the machinery from the beginning. I was adamant that

the bike was a race winner, even when other riders turned their noses up at it, but when it was made really competitive for 1977, I was knocked off the head of the queue to ride it.

After that meeting, Grant thought he had an outside chance of landing the world crown from the five rounds remaining but, although he won the Swedish GP at Anderstorp and was only pipped into second by 0·3 seconds by Walter Villa in the Finnish event at Imatra, numerous problems let him down. What the little Kawasaki lacked in top speed, it made up in fierce acceleration from tight corners. For a circuit like Francorchamps in the Belgian Ardennes – where a 250 was flat-out for much of the $8\frac{3}{4}$ miles – a well-prepared Yamaha would have the edge over the works Kawasaki. But circuits like Assen and Jarama were almost tailor-made for the green machine, because they involve a lot of fierce acceleration between bends and few high-speed straights.

In Belgium, a cut was discovered in the slick Grant had earmarked for the race and he was forced to put on a tyre from the previous meeting, which offered very little grip on the slippery surface. A change to a higher rev band, on the insistence of Grant, played havoc with the power characteristics so that just seven days after his great win in Holland, he finished a disappointing 14th in the Belgian GP.

Although I love road racing, Francorchamps definitely frightens me because it's so fast and slippery. There's never time to collect yourself, although rider ability does count because Walter Villa went past me in 1977 through some of the twisty bits, which made me green with envy – he was so neat.

After so much racing in the United Kingdom, grand prix racing came as a welcome change for Grant and he felt that the switch did wonders for his form.

A run of bad luck which dogged Grant through a troublesome 1978 season appeared to begin with the final two rounds of 1977. First, his front brake stopped functioning when in the leading three in the Czechoslovakian Grand Prix; then, in the final meeting – in Britain, of all places – he fell foul of petty officialdom.

As he and Ditchburn prepared to take their 250 Kawasakis out with the rest of the field for the warm-up lap at Silverstone, they found their way to the track cordoned off. They had arrived a few seconds too late and would have to forgo the all-important warm-up lap.

In Italy, the Italian organisers do their utmost to look after their own riders; in Spain, the Spaniards get the best treatment. Of course, we're completely unique in England in that our federation is fair to the point of frustration rather than looking after anyone British. The last man was just leaving the grid as Ditch and I got to the warm-up enclosure, but they wouldn't let us out. The crowd were going berserk and I'm sure they'd have lynched the officials if they'd got their hands on them.

The Kawasaki always needed a warm-up lap before it would chime properly. Grant's bike limped round on one cylinder on the first lap, came in for a quick plug change and he set off again one lap adrift. He appeared to be making good progress until his machine found a patch of fuel at Copse Corner and he joined several other casualties on the boundary fence.

It was an inauspicious end to a GP season that once promised so much, and the jinx carried on when he campaigned 250 and 350 Kawasaki twins with a new team partner, Kork Ballington, the following year.

Grant had high hopes of landing the world championship in 1978, as had his many thousands of followers throughout Britain and Europe. He had previously had discussions with Suzuki GB and, if Barry Sheene had not re-signed for them, Grant would have been his likely replacement on the works RG500s.

I don't think Barry would have wanted me in the same team and I'm sure Suzuki would not have wanted to afford both of us.

As he was on 12-month contracts with Kawasaki, Grant was entitled to look at all the options, the foundations of his association with Honda being laid before he agreed on a final year with Kawasaki in 1978.

I will not be involved in any mud-slinging, because my four-year relationship with Kawasaki was a good one and, on the whole, a happy one, but there were mistakes made on both sides. To be honest, I wasn't keen to ride 250 and 350 bikes again in 1978. I wanted to get in to the 500cc class but Kawasaki, of course, didn't have the bike. Neither did Honda at that time, so I settled for what Kawasaki had.

I wanted to win a world championship in 1978 so that, hopefully, at the end of the season, I'd be in a position to get a ride on the talked-about 500cc grand prix Honda. That was my plan and I even told Kork what I intended to do. I had lengthy discussions with Honda at the end of 1977 and we agreed that if I had a reasonable season in 1978, we could talk more fully about a Honda for 1979. I must say I was most surprised to finish at the top of their short list after such a disastrous season.

I would always want to leave a factory in such a manner that I could return. As long as you are business-like and your dealings are above board, I think any factory will accept you. But when you're racing at works level, from September to the beginning of January is like musical chairs. If you're still standing when the music stops, you could miss a good ride. There's nothing disloyal or unfair about such talk.

Although he won fewer races at international level with Kawasaki than he did as a privateer, Grant valued his association with the Japanese giant for building him an image.

I realised the problems of people associating my name with nobody else but Kawasaki, which might have made it difficult if I joined another factory.

But, at the time of my switch, Kawasaki had five per cent of the road bike market while Honda had 44 per cent. So although I would lose those who looked upon me as a figurehead for Kawasaki, there would still be a lot of Honda owners able to identify with me, together with those who were genuine Mick Grant fans and who had followed me throughout my career. As long as I did my job right, my following, in theory, should increase.

Honda clearly saw the potential in having such an experienced rider, one with the ability to squeeze the maximum from any machine, to feed back information to factory technicians and, equally important, to project a good image for the team.

When Grant signed the Honda contract, it was a magnificent end to what had been a poor season for him. But he never questioned his own ability, even after a succession of early tumbles and a string of mechanical failures that would have left a weaker man completely dejected. His confidence did ebb at times but, once he established why he was coming off and why there were so many breakdowns, he carried on in the rousing style which the crowds have grown to love.

It was so frustrating to see Kork winning on bikes identical to mine, but my machines just never seemed as quick, especially towards the end of the season.

Tests have proved a disc valve engine like that of the Kawasaki twins is far more critical on carburation than a piston-controlled model such as the 750 Kawasaki triple, which could go from a 540 main jet down to a 460 with no risk of misfire at the top or bottom end. But with a needle only two sizes out on the rotary induction two-stroke, the Kawasaki would not run cleanly.

If it wasn't right, the Kawasaki would accelerate like an old nail. When the bike ran well, the Japanese technician had set the bike up superbly, with the aid of barometers and gauges for measuring the water in the atmosphere; with one eye watching the weather he then would refer to charts to check which jets my bikes wanted. He also had notes from the time when he had designed the engine in the factory. Kork had his brother 'Dozy' working for him as mechanic and he was superb. He had things down to a fine art and if a problem occurred once, it wouldn't happen again. I was unfortunate in that the chap I had, although he was as good as gold, didn't have that same ability. I don't even believe that even Nigel, who has been with me since 1974, had the know-how to do the carburation as successfully as Kork's brother.

Personality clashes amongst riders within factory teams have existed since racing began and a rift can become so wide that one team member will not mind coming second from last as long as he knows his partner is behind him.

In a two-man team one only has to be a little weak for the other to become the dominant figure. Naturally, being friends, as Kork Ballington and I were, helps the team effort considerably, but an alliance between the two men is not vital as long as no dirty linen is being aired in public. Successful sportsmen thrive on competition and having an equally ambitious team-mate on identical machinery will produce a highly competitive racer.

The team manager in a factory outfit must be instrumental in ensuring that the team operates smoothly, whether it's getting spares for the bikes or ironing out problems with the organisers. He should be the hard man of the team. With the success of a team and the promotion of the rider's personality, any manufacturer will sell more motorcycles, so a team manager must establish himself as a strong man when faced with the less pleasant aspects of racing, such as putting in protests to organisers. His job is to run the team on a political basis, not a mechanical one.

When Grant signed for Honda, he reckoned he had another four years racing left in him, although the important thing is, he feels, knowing when to quit.

It's difficult to know when to stop. After a good year when you finish at the top, irrespective of your age, you feel duty bound to continue for another season.

It helps if a factory takes on a rider after he has had a less than highly successful season. By signing a reigning world champion, a manufacturer has everything to lose if it cannot produce a bike capable of allowing him to repeat his success. This will reflect on the motorcycle and not on the racer, who has already proved that he – like the machine he used to be on – was good.

At the time I was making my decision to sign for Honda, I don't think Kawasaki thought I'd leave. When I did break the news, I think they were very surprised. Obviously, we had our ups and downs, but over the four years I reckon it was a very good partnership. The 750 was a fabulous machine to ride. It may not have been the quickest or the best handling bike in racing, but the memories made me sad to see the end of our partnership.

If Kawasaki had produced the machines to continue the challenge, I would have thought seriously about staying.

I had this over-riding feeling that Formula One racing would be very successful and to get a works Honda bike for that class was the same

Kenny Roberts wins the 1978 French GP 500 race in classic style!

as landing a works 500 RG Suzuki when they first appeared. It was so much above anything else. Being involved in the 500cc grand prix effort and in at the start of the swing to four-strokes was also too exciting a proposition to turn down. Whether it was competitive or not, it would be fabulous to ride a four-stroke in the grands prix from the start of the new era. Although success is the aim of all racers, what was more important to me was the belief in my own heart that Honda were doing the right thing.

It's like the guy who turns to religion – he does it for no other reason than a sudden decision that it's something he wants to do. The feeling was so strong inside me that, if I was able to gaze inside a crystal ball and could see that the Honda grand prix machine was going to be a disaster, I still wouldn't have shied away. Of course, I also knew that I would get an awful lot of publicity from racing the Honda.

Although its performance was to be eclipsed by rival factory machines, Grant will always hold his 750cc three cylinder Kawasaki in high regard. Had the machine been more reliable with fewer crankshaft failures (which prevented it finishing many 200-mile races), he was confident that it would have won a 750 world championship title. In 1975, most reckoned it to be the best 750 in the world – but it always seemed to dislike long distances.

When the 650cc Suzukis and 750 Yamahas proved more powerful at the end of Grant's reign with Kawasaki, he felt it could still have matched them with a further 15 bhp spread over the power band. Another suggestion was to bore out the triple to 900cc, which would have given it the extra poke needed to stay with the others for the Superbike series. As it was, the 120 bhp long-stroke Kawasaki still managed joint second place in Europe's most prized competition for large capacity machines in 1978, although Grant's vast experience of the bike's quirks and his circuit knowledge were decisive factors.

The 750 was a brilliant piece of engineering. In 1975 it was a year ahead of its time; by 1978, it was two years behind. Any 750 two-stroke now needs four cylinders to obtain the necessary horsepower.

When Grant joined Kawasaki in 1974, his first job was to see what the green and white machine was capable of. Judging from its early unreliability record, it seemed not a lot. But after the compression ratio had been considerably lowered it was a much better proposition, winning Snetterton's annual Races of Aces and setting a new lap record at the Norfolk circuit.

That year also marked Grant's first appearance on the 750cc air-cooled Kawasaki, an awesome two-stroke beast that was later to capture the TT headlines. In TT practice in 1974, he was taking the device round at 105 mph, but on race day the wet weather

A mono-shock 750cc four-cylinder Yamaha was a popular machine to own in the 1970s for those Superbike riders unfortunate enough not to have a works contract with Suzuki. The drinks can to the right of the engine was there to collect water overflowing from the radiator

Naked – the 750cc water-cooled three-cylinder Kawasaki which Grant rode to many memorable victories

posed a particular problem for Grant, still handicapped by his plaster-encased right wrist. As there was no tyre then made to assist handling in the wet, the big Kawasaki suffered from massive wheelspin and Grant struggled to roll off the power quickly enough on certain sections.

I had no option but to ride it at a very sedate pace. In fact, I went so slowly that I had to stop in the pits to change plugs which had oiled up.

He also led the 750 giants of the time – Canadian Yvon Duhamel and Britain's Paul Smart – at Silverstone; the ignition packed up, but it seemed that there was a future for the machine.

Although tempted by an offer to ride a

'works' Yamaha, imported by Irish dealer Danny Keany, Grant decided to ride the Kawasaki because he felt he would be in a strong position when a European team was formed the following year.

My trouble up to then – and I guess others have suffered in the same way – was that I had worn so many colours and had ridden such a variety of machines. Although I was reasonably popular, I wasn't as recognisable as I was later when I was associated with Kawasaki. I was desperately keen to be associated with one particular marque instead of being a Jack-of-all-bikes.

Grant could see a brighter, long-term career with Kawasaki, who appeared to be on

pionship, then the major championship in Europe outside the world series. In spite of early gearbox and crankshaft troubles, the two-man team of Grant and Barry Ditchburn – backed by a hand-picked team of mechanics and a team manager – virtually swept all before them. Only Suzuki's Barry Sheene offered any real resistance to the Kawasaki challenge, but he was hampered by severe injuries sustained in a 180 mph crash at Daytona.

So what was it like to be transformed from a mere privateer to a famous works rider – at the age of 30?

Very satisfying, although it felt like a natural progression. As a works rider, I never felt any pressure on me from anyone. Anyway, most pressure on people is of their own making. It doesn't matter if you start at 6 or 26 – the average person has between 5 and 15 years of competitive spirit in him. The reason why many motorcycle racers are finished in their early 30s is because they started when they were 17. They have just had enough mentally.

How slickly the Japanese concerns operate was shown by the time it took Kawasaki to sort out a major gearbox fault which had become apparent in the opening Daytona meeting of 1975. Within 14 days, completely re-designed gearboxes had been flown to the UK.

I compared it with the John Player Nortons, which had bad gearboxes from the first day they were raced to the last, if the reports I read were right. It didn't impress me that Kawasaki gearboxes were spitting bits out, but I was impressed that the factory was doing something about it and that – in spite of its massive size – it was adaptable enough to sort out this problem.

They were a new team aiming to set a new image and I was going to grow with them. It wasn't merely a case of having to follow in the shoes of another rider.

Grant was number one rider in that first year, which meant that he got the ride in the event of a machine shortage.

Knowing the success Duhamel had had in the United States with the air-cooled version, Grant was confident the II2R would be a winner. It was the lightest big racing machine in the world and had the edge on the once all-conquering Suzuki three. The bike's weakness was its unreliability through crankshaft failure, but this was gradually sorted out.

By winning the Superbike Championship, amongst many other outstanding performances, Grant feels that they did too well that season, which discouraged Kawasaki from putting in the required effort to stay at the top in the following year. Suzuki was able to regain the racing whip-hand, which meant that Barry Sheene was still the number one rider in Britain.

the verge of making a big racing effort. He became a full-time Kawasaki works rider on January 1, 1975 and over the next four years, riding the same remarkable 750, he took scores of victories and broke lap records throughout the United Kingdom. Even more important to the factory, Grant did more than anything to further the name of the marque: Big K had arrived in Britain and Grant was the number one preacher of the Japanese gospel!

With the new factory-supplied 750 fitted with a six-speed instead of a five-speed gearbox, a lighter, better-handling chassis and more horsepower, priority in the first year was the *Motor Cycle News* Superbike Cham-

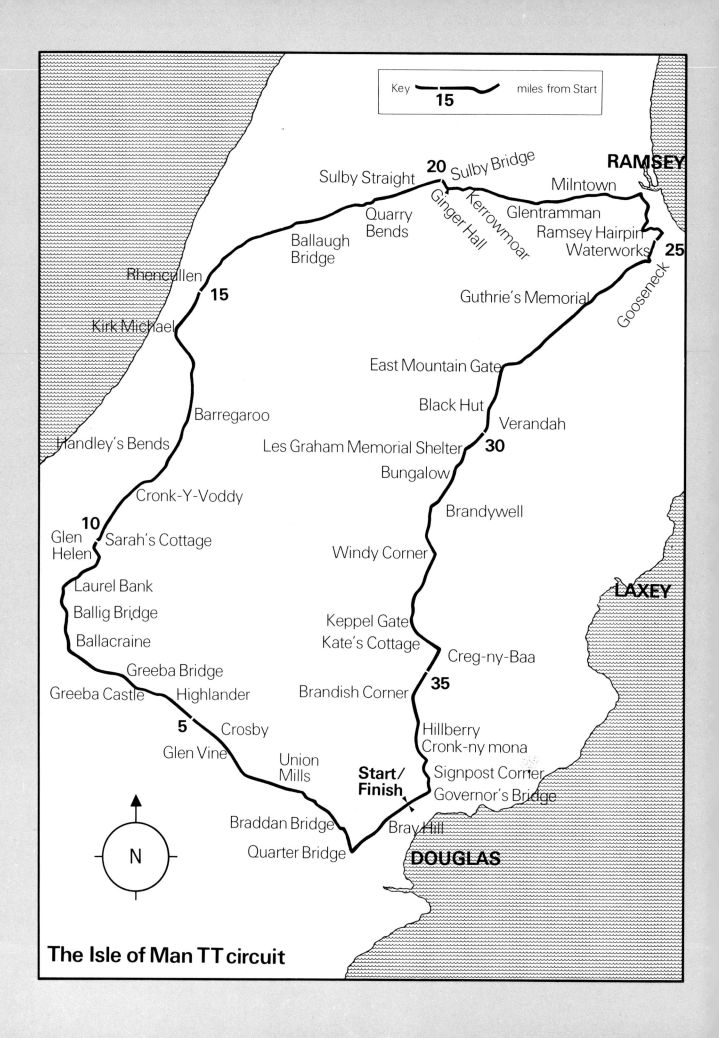

The Isle of Man TT circuit

LAPPING THE TT CIRCUIT

To race round the 37¾ miles of the Isle of Man Mountain Circuit is regarded by all those who have done it as the greatest experience a road racer can enjoy. No one circuit has aroused so much interest, so helped to develop machines or transformed so many boys into men as this amazing natural course, whose history and traditions have filled the pages of books and periodicals throughout the world.

As long as machines become faster every year and riders exist with the expertise to control them, the absolute TT lap record will know no reasonable limit. More than anything else, Mick Grant's circuit knowledge has helped him to break records on the Island: his incredible memory of every wiggle, fall and rise of the road cannot be rivalled.

An imaginary flying lap of the TT course on a six-speed 750cc machine – capable of 190 mph – calls for brilliant thinking, split-second timing and spine-chilling courage. Maximum speeds for each gear would normally be: first – 70 mph; second – 95; third – 115; fourth – 130; fifth – 165; and sixth 180 to 190 mph.

I have always believed that the purpose of racing is to discover a combination of yourself and machine which is the best in any particular race. The trick is getting that combination exactly right.

The combination of myself and the Kawasaki was a formidable one although I say so myself. The bike was right for the Isle of Man and I like the Isle of Man – it was the perfect marriage. The Kawasaki had a nice spread of power in 1978, with a power band starting at 7,000 rpm and finishing at 9,500 rpm and I can honestly say that for 80 per cent of the time in the Island, the rev counter needle didn't go above 8,500 rpm.

If I had ridden the Kawasaki to maximum revs in every gear, I would have been three miles per hour slower, because there would have been too much power for me. There were places where I was changing gear at 8,000 rpm, hardly on the power band, and it would pull nice and softly. I could be cranked right to the limit, change up and still be accelerating; if I had been going to 9,500 on the same corner and giving it stick, the back end would have been bucking.

The successful TT rider's thoughts before the clutch start centre on one objective – to get down the stretch of road ahead perfectly – and it's not just a question of speed.

If you make a balls-up of the start through either wheel-spin or by lifting the front wheel of the bike on the stretch to Bray Hill, you will have great difficulty getting past the guy you've set off with until well past Quarter Bridge. You can make up so much time in those early stages of the first lap. To lose three or four seconds at the beginning would call for much more effort to get back later in the race.

On a flying lap, however, Grant crosses the start and finish line in fifth, tight against the right-hand wall to get a good swing at the left-hander under the footbridge. Care has to be taken over a bump by the traffic lights, which could lead to a weave. Down bumpy Bray Hill at high speed, Grant is four feet from the left gutter.

I have heard tales of riders going down Bray Hill flat out, but I hook it down to fifth. Coming out, you must almost clip the right-hand kerb.

Any gear higher than fourth or fifth will kill the engine on the climb out of Bray Hill. The object there is to keep both wheels on the ground, instead of the classic Agostini pose of a spectacular wheelie, which just attracts wind resistance with the larger frontal area.

On the approach to Quarter Bridge, still in fifth gear, a blind left-hand corner with adverse camber calls for a total reduction in power and he goes round on the over-run. The braking point for the sharp right-hander at Quarter Bridge means bikes spilling their load from full fuel tanks, making control even more difficult on cold tyres. Grant takes it cautiously in first gear.

Not timing the braking right, as I have done on occasions, means you go over the round-about – it's fascinating to see how quickly the large crowd parts when you just manage to stop with your front wheel against the netting by the pub. You understand how Moses felt when he saw the Red Sea parting!

Then it's up to fourth before braking heavily and changing down into first for the left-hand bend at Braddan Bridge; then into second as the S-bend is completed by running near to the churchyard wall. There's a sharp left-hand bend half-way to Union Mills which is taken flat out in fifth.

Union Mills is wider than it was and you can go into it a lot quicker than you really want to. I peel off by the water pipe just before the right-

hander, to get the correct line for the straight after the following left-hander. The bike is shaking about over the bumps, but it's a fabulous sensation taking the big sweep out of Union Mills. It's one of the most important corners on the circuit. Come out five miles an hour quicker than your opponent and you hold that advantage for up to a mile over the long straight which follows.

Nearing Glen Vine, the bike is dropped back into fifth. The road at that point seems narrower than it really is, so you have to throw the bike into the bend unusually early; at the speed I'm travelling, it feels like 30 yards before the actual bend.

On the straight past the Crosby Hotel, especially if the wind is not in my favour, I knock it down to fifth and, on the hill before the Highlander Inn, the bike tends to come off the floor. By going two feet from the right-hand gutter, where the road is slightly lower, the machine can be kept almost on the deck without rolling off the power.

Then, usually with a tail wind, it's along the fastest part past the Highlander (where a speed trap was once sited). Every movement has to be made hundreds of yards prior to a bend to eliminate sudden swerves, which waste time as well as being dangerous. Even so, you can see the drinkers at the Highlander with their pint glasses; if the machine is going to miss a beat, you wish it were there.

At Greeba Castle, where orthodox lines are called for, the bike is put into third, although Grant feels it gets too close to the bales at the exit for comfort. He once fell off here in practice and felt hurt all over.

Through Appledene, Greeba Bridge and past the Hawthorn Inn – sometimes in fifth, other times in top – and on towards Ballacraine, where the first Manx Radio commentary point is manned by ex-racer Tommy Robb. The biggest problem at Ballacraine is finding a braking marker on the fast run into the right-hander.

On the exit, I like to have my wheels jammed up against the wall of the pub and it's a comforting thought to know there is nowhere for the wheels to slide.

The famous points of the course go flashing by – Ballig Bridge, Ballaspur, Doran's Bend, each requiring a special line. Grant's first signal point is in a gateway 30 yards past Laurel Bank, where he is accelerating at 80 mph – slow enough to read the details.

Past the Esso garage on the right – through a very tricky left and a right-hand corner – cutting the left much tighter to be faster coming out of the right-hander. Then it's flat stick to Glen Helen, knock it down a gear without touching the brakes and take it down to second over the small bridge; a wide sweep round the dip and up the hill, being careful of the adverse camber when feeding in the power or the back

end might come round, although there is a nice solid bank to stop you if you come off. Then up to third, back down to second and stamp on the brake for the right-hander at Sarah's Cottage; feed the power in gently and change up into third to make it pull rather than rev onto the Cronk-y-voddy straight. Now I'm really flying, so I get into the right-hand gutter to stop the bike jumping too high in the air – two jumps can be reduced to one big one with extra speed. The next bit is not so bumpy and I can go flat out in top, but it returns to bumps where the re-surfacing finishes at the crossroads. At the blind brow, the road dives right down to the 11th milestone – miss the corner and you go through the hedge, so knock the power off to prevent the bike leaping.

Every inch of the way there's something to remember but, for Grant, each stretch can be tackled with confidence, knowing precisely which side of the road he should be on, the ideal speed and gear.

After Handley's Cottage and a swooping left-hander before the straight at the top of Barregarroo, Grant finds the approach to Barregarroo crossroads terrifying. As with Glen Vine, the course here seems to shrink in width because of the pace.

What frightens me is the nice long straight beforehand, which gives you time to wonder what's going to happen when you get there. So easy to make a mistake there.

On the run-down to Barregarroo, the experienced spectators listen for the brave riders – the ones who don't ease back the throttle on the 750s. Grant does.

In the dip, everything bottoms, the exhausts are likely to be bashed and the bike can wobble for quite a distance coming out of the corner, all of which makes this Grant's favourite point when he has a chance to watch the action.

The road sweeps into Kirkmichael village, where any delay in braking will plunge the rider into a house wall. The buildings on either side echo the noise of the bike and give the rider a terrific sensation of speed.

Kirkmichael is like one of these 'test-your-skill' machines at the fair, where the ribbon of track weaves from side to side and you have to steer the make-believe car along the middle of the track.

By the service station before Rhencullen is one of the dangerous stretches for the unwary. A low sun at certain times dazzles the rider and the risk of shunting another rider or of misjudging the right-hander is high.

Rhencullen, Bishopscourt (with its aroma of wild garlic) and then Ballaugh Bridge – a popular spot for photographers. Grant's riding style in the TT has changed completely from his Yamaha days at places like this. Whereas he once leapt Ballaugh Bridge with three feet to spare, a factory commitment

makes him treat the jump far more cautiously nowadays, with the emphasis on finishing the race rather than striving only for a new lap record.

He believes the only way the hump-back Ballaugh Bridge should be tackled is to land on the front wheel, because it saves the transmission and allows braking to be left to the last minute. .

You have to be practical about somewhere like Ballaugh or anywhere that it's possible to look spectacular. Better to be safe than showy. This business about giving it a blip and landing on the back wheel is bullshit. That automatically puts a lot of tension on the gearbox, chain and suspension. Landing on the front wheel does tend to suggest it's hairy and a bit out of control, mind you. In 1972, the commentator at Ballaugh, Geoff Cannell, told the fans he thought I was going to crash every time. It sounded really bad and I knew that the John Player Norton team manager, Frank Perris, was hearing this in the pits. If he thinks I'm a lunatic, I thought, there's no way I'll get a ride on the John Player Norton.

Never one to take matters lying down, Grant took advantage of a lull during practice to visit Cannell in his elevated position and explain why he chose to land front-end first over Ballaugh. Grant wanted Cannell to refrain from suggesting that he was riding in a wild manner at that point; but the commentator – now a friend of the Yorkshireman – insisted he would describe Grant's style over the bridge in any way he wanted. And he would say it was hairy!

The following event saw Grant tackling Ballaugh in very unfamiliar fashion. Hurrying through on the first lap, he jumped it in Grant style – nose down; next time, when leading handsomely, he did it in classic Agostini style, with the bike at 45 degrees to the vertical for Cannell's benefit. On the third lap, with a 90-second lead, he went over without the wheels leaving the ground and stuck two fingers up at the bemused commentator to tell him that he had now negotiated the bridge in every possible way. A few miles further on, with no flag warning given, Grant embarrassingly and angrily came adrift on a patch of oil at Ramsey and was out.

Cannell initially thought Grant's sign was one of victory by a confident man, only to be told later what the rider had really meant!

With Ballaugh out of the way, riders pass Gwen, the kindly lady to whom they traditionally wave as she stands by the gate of her white house. Between races or practice sessions, no rider would ever dare pass her house without dropping in for a cup of tea. Inside are cuttings and pictures of TT riders from years gone by. Gwen was upset when Agostini once described her as 'the old woman in a white coat'!

above
Two ways of jumping Ballaugh Bridge in the Isle of Man. Grant prefers the front wheel landing to minimise strain on the rear wheel, suspension, chain and transmission

right
Trouble at the TT. Grant parts company with his Yamaha at Parliament Square in Ramsey when leading

opposite
Past the Keppel Hotel and onto the TT circuit's fastest stretch goes Grant on the 750cc Kawasaki during his victorious 1978 Classic TT ride

Then it is on in top gear towards Quarry Bends – where the bike can try to tie itself into a knot when carrying a lot of fuel – and onto the bumpy Sulby Straight where, on full power, the machine can be pitched almost vertically onto its rear wheel beside the pub half-way along.

Glentramman follows Ginger Hall and Kerrowmoar and there is a stretch of road just before Milntown that is notorious for flies. Grant always thinks about the consequences of colliding with a dog at that point, remembering the time when a competitor did just that in the 1970s. The dog shot out of a hedge and the rider hit it flat-out in top gear.

At Schoolhouse Bend there is a bump so bad that Grant has actually tried the left side of the road to miss it, although this puts him completely off line for the left-hander.

It's bumps like that some people want removed, but it should remain – it's all part of riding the circuit.

After Parliament Square in Ramsey, May Hill sees the start of what Grant regards as the second section of the TT Circuit. The first part is the flat section from the start to Ramsey, followed by the Mountain Climb and then the last section, the descent back to the finish line, a stretch which Grant considers his best of the three.

May Hill is one of the most deceptive corners of the lot; you have been travelling so fast for so long that it's very hard to judge speed on slow corners such as this.

After Ramsey hairpin, where it is still common for riders to overshoot despite it being uphill, come the Waterworks and the Gooseneck, where Grant has his next signal board.

He freewheels into the Gooseneck and, with the engine just on the power band, begins to feed in the throttle. This way, by eliminating the clutch, there will be no time-wasting 'wheelies'.

Just prior to the Mountain Mile is the bend Grant rates as the most important on the whole circuit – a right-hander over a bridge.

Get over that bridge just a bit quicker than your opponent and you can make a couple of seconds on him at the end of the Mountain Mile, which you take flat-out on a 750. Do that corner better than anyone else and you can sit on your arse for over a mile and reap the rewards.

The four right-hand kinks at the Verandah are taken as one sweep, although mistaking the third one for the last can put the rider very close to the edge of the road and set the heart fluttering. They look so similar that Grant counts them off to ensure he is correctly on line at the exit.

After the Les Graham memorial, where the road surface reverts to the original bumpy texture which Grant much prefers, he brakes hard for the Bungalow as soon as he sees the directional marker arrow – a tip he first read in literature supplied to him as a newcomer to the Island.

Grant then speeds up towards Brandywell, taking second gear through the aptly-named Windy Corner, where sharp gusts can buffet the machine, and then on to Keppel Gate, which he feels is the real start of the downhill run back to the finish.

The little kink going down the Mountain at Kate's Cottage is a terrifying one. Because you're going very hard and there are high banks, you breathe a sigh of relief every time you get through it.

The road down to Creg-ny-Baa is the straightest on the Island and – just before the jump halfway along – Grant changes up to fifth to prevent his bike from becoming air-borne.

If you're not careful you can be rushing into the right-hander at the Creg much quicker than you want to and with the high bankings either side and the road appearing to become narrower all the time with the increasing speed, it's like travelling down the inside of a drainpipe.

The two hardest braking points in the TT are into Creg-ny-Baa and at Brandish, where the rider is braking downhill from 185 mph into first or second gear. As wind often whistles through gateways on either side, the trick is to take a middle line down the rush to Brandish to avoid being blown off line.

Grant likes to brake very late indeed for Brandish, before the next straight to Hil-berry. Once past this point, he senses that another lap is almost over. There is still Cronk-ny-Mona and Signpost to contend with before Bedstead, but the short bends leading to the Nook and the slowest corner of all – at Governor's Bridge – offer little opportunity to make up time.

As he leaves the Dip, he brushes the wall on his left and is careful not to wheelie the machine over a bump upon hitting the Glen-crutchery Road, again to save the precious split-seconds which can mean the difference between a lap record and an average time.

I have the worst memory in the world, but when it comes to the Isle of Man I can remember every bump. I may forget some of the place names but, if asked to pinpoint pot-holes or man-holes or even the start of a different road surface, I can give an answer almost straight away. What it proves is that my mind is lazy – I remember only what I want to remember.

The feeling as I cross the line first is one I never get in any other race in the world. I'm really racing myself to see if I can improve my time from the previous year, especially if I'm on the same tackle. If I'm 12 seconds faster than the year before, irrespective of where I've finished, I say to myself: 'I've beaten the old Mick Grant' and, funnily enough, that gives me a lot of satisfaction.

THE ISLE OF MAN

THE ISLE OF MAN

opposite
Grant descends the Mountain in the 1973 F750 TT, during his second-placed ride on the John Player Norton

While he has proved himself on tracks all over the world, much of Grant's reputation as a racer has been built on his brilliant performances in the Isle of Man. Although he has raised the absolute lap record with almost every visit, the 1975 TT stands out for all the wrong reasons: on one of its infrequent outings, the 500cc Kawasaki took him to a most unexpected victory in the wet Senior after the machine had seized within a mile of the start! With the clutch in and coasting through the roundabout at Quarter Bridge with his race apparently over, Grant decided to motor the complete lap back to the pits to give the thousands of spectators a glimpse of the bike.

He was revving to 9,000 rpm, just on the power band, as he circulated none too seriously. Then to his surprise he was signalled as holding fourth place. He couldn't believe it but, just in case the information was right and as the motor showed no signs of seizing again, he decided to keep going. It ran without trouble for five laps and, knowing there would be little chance of a repeat seizure by that time, Grant really turned up the wick for the last 37¾ miles to snatch victory and the fastest lap of 102·93 mph.

In the long gap between the end of warming-up and the start of the race, the engine had gone really cold in the wet, miserable conditions and my blasting it away from the start just seized it. The pistons had swelled up while the cylinders hadn't. But I really gave it some welly on that final lap.

This 500 triple, on which Grant had earlier scooped the North-West 200 road circuit event in Ulster (on a double victory day, as he became the first ever to lap a British circuit at more than two miles a minute on his 750) was later given to Lord Montagu for display at the Beaulieu National Motor Museum. Apart from three major wins in Grant's hands, however, it was far from competitive and Kawasaki, following some grand prix failures with it, were not keen on developing it at that stage.

It was quite a nice machine to ride apart from being very revvy, but it wasn't a lot quicker than a 350 Yamaha. It felt so wide with its three cylinders in a row, when I had been used to the narrow configurations of the Yamaha, Commando and the Goldie, that it was akin to sitting on a double-decker bus.

In fact, the bike was little changed from the

following page
Over-eagerness by Grant caused this spill involving Keith Heckles at Signpost Corner in the 1971 F750cc TT. Both men were unhurt. The exhaust pipes on Grant's Lee Commando, by the way, were deliberately painted orange to attract attention

500cc Padgett Kawasaki which Grant had ridden to third place in the 1972 Senior TT, apart from the addition of a water-jacket and disc brakes.

But the big capacity race always remains the most popular spectacle in the Isle of Man; when Grant shattered the existing lap record with a speed of 109·82 mph on his 750cc triple, the crowd whooped with delight – Mike Hailwood's record had stood for eight years. But Grant's joy turned to disaster when the bike's chain snapped at the exit from the Gooseneck while he was comfortably in the lead.

The hammering the Kawasaki took proved too much for the Renold chain. The course is so bumpy that the suspension is working to capacity all the time: with the back wheel off the road so much, the revs shoot up. Then the wheel hits the road again and the wheel centre can be going twice as fast as the road speed, which puts a tremendous strain on all the mechanical components and on the tyres. On a normal circuit, the bike just isn't subjected to that sort of pressure.

We knew from the start that there could well be a transmission problem. My plan, as it always is in the TT, was to break the opposition on the first couple of laps and build a good lead. That seems to be the best technique over there. I did this according to plan, but the chain had been jumping a bit. Experience told me to nurse the bike home but, the chain still broke. I was keen to do well and the extra power I was putting on was enough to snap the chain.

Everyone was clapping the new record as I walked back, but it didn't mean a thing to me at the time. What mattered was winning that race, an opportunity I had been denied. Looking back, breaking the record was definitely a bonus because it captured people's imaginations, but I can remember saying to myself: 'What are all these guys getting excited about just because I've broken a lap record'.

Since then I have realised a lap record in the Isle of Man is more important than winning a race, one of the crazy things that the press must be blamed for building up. Winning at the slowest possible speed is the only proper attitude to take but the first time I come away from the Isle of Man without a lap record I'll be worse off for it.

I didn't use a Renold chain again until the 1978 TT, when it worked perfectly. It was covered in a new super lubricant and didn't

even need adjusting after the race. This is why places like the Isle of Man are so important for machine development, because that fault would never have shown itself anywhere else and the lubricant would never have been discovered.

When Grant finally cracked Mike Hailwood's absolute TT lap record in 1975 many critics of modern riders asked why it had taken so long in view of the faster bikes and better road surfaces.

Since the record was set in 1967, there had not been the intense competition in the Isle of Man by factory teams. Prior to that, all the stars were there because they needed world championship points. That competition made riders go quicker. When the big names stayed away, for one reason or another, competition died off. Those who have ridden there since have had the ability but perhaps not the incentive. There were also several years when bad weather kept speeds down. I know that when I won the 1975 Senior, my fastest lap was only 102 mph because it was wet. The weather has to be just right to get the big laps.

When Hailwood retired, Agostini was winning the lot on 350cc and 500cc MV Agustas; in the TT, he was only racing against Manx Nortons and Matchless G50s. And when the 750s came out, they presented difficult handling problems. One has to remember that the Honda which Mike Hailwood rode to the record in 1967, although a bit of a camel, was giving out the sort of horsepower that we get in 750s now. After MV pulled out, what bikes were there to set a new record?

Because it had a road engine it would be no use suggesting the John Player Norton was capable of setting a new TT lap record. It just couldn't be compared with the specially-prepared four-cylinder Honda. The Commando was kicking out just 68 horsepower at 7,000 rpm – when it didn't spit its guts out – and for Peter Williams to get round at 107 mph on it was an incredible performance. It took until the mid-1970s for the 350cc Yamahas to come good there once more: when I did 104 mph on a 350 in 1974, the Yamahas were just starting to get going again.

Bill Ivy went round at an amazing 100·32 mph in 1968 on a 125 Yamaha on bumpy roads, so the engines then must have been something special. I know Bill was a great rider but he also had the competition to make him go quicker. In the four years I rode the big Kawasaki in the TT, my speeds slowly went up – partly because of the improved road surface, partly because of the tyres but, more than anything else, because of the competition.

When I did the 114·33 mph lap, I was going about as quickly as I could to stay on the machine, yet on the same motorcycle against stiffer competition, because of human nature, I could have gone a little faster.

The ones who make it in this game are those who are turned on by competition.

The disastrous 1976 TT was Grant's most forgettable. After achieving a 110 mph lap in practice, which earned him lots of publicity for becoming the first to hit that figure in TT history, little else went right for him.

He never got to grips with the strange-handling 500 and, when it seized on the second lap of the Senior, no-one was more relieved than Grant.

Stan Woods said that when he passed me at Schoolhouse, my bike was going sideways.

In the Isle of Man, Grant feels that good handling is far more important than horsepower. The extra-large fuel tank the 500-3 was carrying that year was thought to have had a detrimental effect on the bike's handling.

When it came to the big-money, six-lap Classic race, on the other hand, Grant had never felt more confident.

Occasionally, for no reason at all, you know at the start that you're going to win; when I get that feeling, although it might make me a little nervous, it very rarely fails. But this happened to be one time it didn't come right.

Such was his confidence that he stood the big 750 on its rear wheel (to the delight of the crowd) as he rocketed along the Glencrutchery Road for the first time. Just half a mile further and the clutch began to slip at the bottom of Bray Hill. Grant was dismayed, because he knew that his mechanic Nigel Everett had double-checked everything before the start and that the preparation was, literally, faultless. Hoping it might be oil on the clutch, he wanted to get it hot to see if the plates would start to grip again. The slip was just as intense at Ballacraine, however, so he stopped to see if he could borrow tools to make an adjustment.

Everyone at Ballacraine was goggle-eyed with surprise to see me pull in and no-one was actually moving to get any tools. So I thought 'sod it' and set off again. I knew I'd either melt the clutch or it would go right.

As he went through Doran's Bend and Laurel Bank he imagined the clutch improving but it began to deteriorate again in third and fourth gears, making it an almost hopeless task and forcing him to retire.

No circuit in the world has attracted more criticism over its safety than the Isle of Man, although the loudest noises to remove the event from the racing calendar often come from those who fail to attend the fortnight's feast of speed.

Everything has its critics, but each circuit is only as dangerous as you make it. I don't think the Isle of Man is dangerous. One point I will concede is at the bottom of Bray Hill: if the bike goes bang there or the forks drop off, then there's a good chance you'll hurt yourself. And if a handlebar broke at the top of Barregarroo,

opposite
Grant accelerates hard out of Ballacraine to take the 500cc three-cylinder Kawasaki to victory in the 1975 Senior TT

I wouldn't give much for your chances. People may laugh when I say I always go round the Island with a little bit in reserve, but that's the safety factor. There's no way I'll ever say I won't crash over there because I have done.

I treat the Island with a lot more respect than, say, a short circuit that's relatively safe. That's human nature and that's why it's a safe circuit.

I never cease to be amazed that people can be so naive as to suggest the Isle of Man is out-dated when considering today's modern machinery. Those who have never ridden motorcycles which do 180 mph think that life must be a big blur at that speed, with no possible chance of being able to see. But you can see just as well at 180 as you can at 130. Why should speed be a frightening factor?

When Mac Hobson and Kenny Birch died in the 1978 TT, it wasn't the bump at the top of Bray Hill that killed them. The bump was there to be ridden – or avoided. They made a mistake – we all can – by not going to one side of it. The bumps actually make racing safer, because they help to reduce speeds.

By wanting to take each bump out to appease someone, the next move would be to take out another bump further on. There would be no end to it and £20 million would be spent making the TT circuit the same as Paul Ricard. The whole idea of the TT, or for any real road cir-cuit, is that the rider takes on the circuit and I just cannot understand why some riders want it as smooth as a billiard table.

When I first started, the Laurel Bank section was bumpy, which would put you in a permanent – but safe – tank-slapper. The fastest and slowest riders would have their bikes twitching and just how much the back end and handlebars twitched depended on how fast you wanted to go. Now it's dead smooth, riders are going round it ten miles an hour faster and the first time you realise you've made a mistake is when the back end steps out of line and you're down.

The enjoyment of the TT for spectators isn't just the racing. It's getting there, the early morning practice and everything surrounding the magical fortnight. Every year, thousands of residents accept the fact that someone will be rushing through at four in the morning and perhaps frightening them out of their wits. An outsider wouldn't believe that until he actually saw it.

More riders enjoy the TT than don't, but I would never criticise any rider for not wanting to ride in the TT, no matter what his reason. But I cannot understand how people who say they love racing motorbikes cannot enjoy racing a bike round the Isle of Man. I get a lot of satisfaction from riding round somewhere like Mallory Park, which is just a simple speed-bowl. But the pleasure to be derived from the Isle of Man is completely different. There's the challenge of racing on the open roads; with the TT riders starting off at ten-second intervals, the challenge is you against the clock rather than against another rider, which makes the TT a far more personal thing.

If the Mountain Circuit wasn't so long, it wouldn't be so controversial and wouldn't have lasted as long as it has done. We know the Isle of Man is different, that's why it fills so many column inches in journals throughout the world. Motorcycle racing would definitely be poorer without it.

Clearly, many of those who don't go are not absentees through choice. They just cannot afford to go. If some feel they don't want to go racing in the Island, that's their decision and no-one should criticise them for having the courage of their convictions. No-one thinks any worse of Barry Sheene for not wanting to go; he certainly doesn't lose any sleep over his decision to stay away. You're either for or against Sheene, as was the case with Read. Perhaps Barry has been clever, knowing he will get more publicity by staying away than by actually riding there. As long as he is convinced he is doing the right thing that's all that matters.

The TT is an event that can live on its own. The best thing that ever happened to it was when it lost its world championship status. People once had to go there for the points, even though they might have hated it. For the young promising fireball, the TT did little for his world championship bid: to go round safely

would take him three years. Someone with a good memory and good style might take only two years, but the average guy would take three years before he started to go quickly. I know it took me three years.

Now, without championship status, the organisers can put on the races they want to put on, the races the public want to see and which provide much better entertainment altogether. Whether that's actually being done now is open to debate, but at least the event does not depend on a world championship run by the FIM. As long as it retains its classic dates, it will attract a following of people from Bognor Regis to Bonn, who always book their holiday dates for that period.

I am a simple country lad at heart, so if people tell me they don't go to the Island because they think it's too dangerous, then I'll believe them. Of course, Phil Read used to say it was dangerous. What I think he meant was that he was not getting enough money. But he did enjoy riding there – you could tell that just by watching him go round. When I watched him on his private Yamaha at Brandywell in 1972, he was absolutely superb, head and shoulders above everyone. So I couldn't understand why he rubbished the TT the following year.

He went back because of a combination of riding enjoyment and finance, which outweighed any potential dangers. When he finally did quit, there was only the enjoyment to balance against the danger.

Had the TT paid the sort of money it's doing now, it would not have lost its world championship status. With a £6,000 first prize, it would have attracted the topliners all the time. That's a fact.

But money is still far from being the life-blood of the TT because so many riders compete each year without making a penny. Most, in fact, lose money.

When machines have spent a tough fortnight of practising and racing at the TT, they are more or less worn out – most riders reckon the demands on machinery are the equivalent of half a season of short circuit racing.

When start money was first paid, it didn't attract dozens of new faces. It merely meant riders could afford to go, although quite a number of racers could still make more money by contesting several internationals elsewhere.

The top professional is still losing money by going: he could earn his TT start money fee several times over by cramming in three or four other meetings and he wouldn't subject his bikes to so much wear and tear.

Although I don't have to be switched on by cash, as a professional I couldn't afford to go if the money wasn't there. My love of the sport is great, but professionals still have to look at it as a business and it can be very difficult to keep the two objectives in perspective.

The TT now offers thousands of pounds in

103

prize money, making it the richest meeting in the world, and Grant sees a secure future for the event over the next few seasons, after lean years when it was snubbed by the top names for a variety of reasons, most involving circuit dangers. Daily newspapers made capital out of the ever-growing fatality count and it was the death tally that drew the fiercest criticism every time the TT was discussed at the annual congress of the governing Federation Internationale Motorcycliste.

Statistics can make black appear as white, so I don't set so much store by them but I do feel the Isle of Man could reduce the number of accidents.

The hot-blooded kids have to learn road circuits somewhere, but using the Island as a training ground is really jumping in at the deep end. They should try some of the fabulous Irish road races, which include eight-lap events where they can get the feel of the bike bouncing off the floor. Irish road racing can help to train people for the TT if they want to do it seriously.

Grant thinks a quarter of a mile ahead of the bike in the TT, planning his bends to ensure that he is on the right line every time. In a six-lap race, he might be just off the line once and even that might not be on his own making – as happened in the 1978 Classic, when his suspension bottomed coming out of Quarry Bends and threw him three feet off line.

The average professional can go to the Island and ride safely; it's the novices who worry me. That's why I worry about the Manx Grand Prix, which is potentially more dangerous than the TT.

Grant wants to see the TT slimmed down to cater for the real professionals, riders of equal calibre, to the exclusion of 'holiday' racers on their annual visit to the Island.

Someone who gets on a bike once or twice a year is not only sticking his neck out but is a danger to other competitors. The sport is now so competitive that you have to be riding regularly and it's unforgivable to allow someone to don his leathers once a year just to have a plod around the Isle of Man. There used to be guys who became loonies once they raced on the Island.

The biggest danger in the TT is dealing with riders going too slowly, and who are suddenly encountered in the middle of the road.

Speed never killed anybody – it's people going at different speeds that cause accidents. If we all travelled at the same speed, no-one would be hurt because you wouldn't bump into one another. My heart-stopping moments have all involved slow riders displaying unprofessional conduct. There are guys with their engines misfiring, pottering up the centre of the road looking under the tank when they should be cruising right on the edge of the tarmac – you wouldn't catch an English professional doing

that. Then there are riders in Formula 750 races who pull straight out onto the track after refuelling, without bothering to look before filtering in. God knows what they drive like on the road.

Nobody, of course, is under any obligation to ride beyond their limits on their TT debut, but some top riders are frightened to go because of the risk of being beaten by lesser lights. But the regular TT-goers understand the predicament of racing first-timers and only expect so much in terms of performance.

The knowledgeable TT fans can put it all in perspective – just giving it a try is more important than where you finish. The spectators are quite happy to see a rider learn the TT for a couple of years before becoming competitive. There are those who say they won't go because the TT is dangerous, but if they were truthful they only refuse because they feel they lack the experience to go quickly and people might think worse of them.

But it's not all about winning races on the fastest bike. There should surely be some satisfaction out of riding a motorcycle against the elements. I like the adverse cambers and bumps – it's a circuit with character. If we were to take any circuit, my racing line would be pretty much identical to that of any top rider, but for the Isle of Man, even if we all were on the same bikes, we would each have different lines and that's what makes it so interesting.

One of the men whose inexperience of the Isle of Man cost him dearly was the talented American, Pat Hennen, who was enjoying his best season as a Suzuki GB works rider when he made his second visit to the Island. Grant believes that Hennen may have succumbed to press reports which described how he did 113 mph in practice 'with only 80 per cent effort'.

You may think it's sheer rubbish but there could come a time where you believe what you read and I think Pat fell into the trap of believing very fast lap times were within the grasp of most. I think it was over-confidence.

Hennen lay second to Tom Herron in the 1978 Senior TT and was pulling out all the stops to make up an almost impossible time gap. He lost control of his Suzuki doing 160 mph at Bishopscourt and head injuries put him out of racing for a long time.

He should have used those last two laps to gain more experience and line himself up for a good crack at the 750 race later in the week. Had I been in his place, with Tom on my tail and the time advantage in my rival's favour, there is no way I would even have tried to leave him in a lap. Tom was one of the three or four runners over there from whom you couldn't pull 20 seconds once they had you in their sights.

Apart from fuel stops, I can do six TT laps within four or five seconds of each other if I want to, so a 30-second margin from one lap to another is quite enormous. But at Brands Hatch, even half a second difference per lap is a lifetime. If you're a second a lap slower each time on a 30-lapper at Brands, you're almost ready for being lapped towards the end.

Having said that, because I know the Island so well, I will put in as much effort as I would for Mallory or Brands, but the yellow stripe down my back will only let me go as quickly as is necessary. Somewhere in my mind (perhaps in all racers' minds), there's an automatic fail-safe device which governs my speed.

At a place like Brands, a top rider who had never been there before could go round only seconds off a competitive time within three or four laps. After 20 laps, he'd be going round a second off the time he'd do in the race. But it takes three years to arrive at this stage in the Isle of Man, even if you're sharp.

More than anything else, the TT is all about getting your homework right and, while there are still corners each year I cannot get absolutely right, there's a continual need to improve.

Although the standard is very high, I think it could go even higher if riders put more homework in. I always go to the Isle of Man a fortnight before practice to do a few dozen laps in a car. When I arrive there on the Tuesday of practice week, shattered after the Brands Bank Holiday Monday meeting, I'm actually switched onto the Isle of Man because I was there recently, not 12 months ago like many competitors. That's why I usually manage to equal my previous year's lap record within a few practice laps.

If you're not a natural rider, as in my case, it's part of the job to become familiar with a circuit by walking it and then discussing it with those who know it well. I look out for the bumps, where it's grippy and even beyond the perimeter of the track to see if I could stay on the bike without tumbling if I had to take to the grass. It's positive thinking because, when faced with going into a ditch, it's best to know beforehand whether you'd be better on or off the bike. The confidence this knowledge gives does enable you to go round that little bit quicker.

One of the things that gets me back each year is the thought that I can do better. Each time you do a corner in the Island you feel you could have gone through faster and even if you did the TT until you were 150 years old, you'd never be completely satisfied. By checking other people's lines and constantly practising a certain section where you feel you're not good enough, it can eventually become your best section.

This act of polishing up the weak points rewarded Grant in 1974 when his favourite section was Cronk-ny-Mona, a long series of left-handers before Signpost. On a 350, it could be taken flat-out with the tyres just starting to slide.

Being right on the limit of tyre adhesion was a superb feeling. One mile an hour faster and perhaps you would be off, but to be in control on the very limit sent a charge through the body that nothing else in life could match. Pleasure from any of the other 36 miles would be forgotten just because of that one corner. Come out of the corner knowing you've done it right and that's your own little private ego trip.

But no matter how thorough the preparation has been, there is no guarantee that a bike will start a race, let alone finish it. John Williams, an absolutely brilliant Isle of Man rider (who later lost his life in the 1978 Ulster Grand Prix at Dundrod) felt reasonably confident about winning the £6,000 first prize in the 1977 Classic TT, but as a professional he realised that anything could stand in the way of his taking the richest race in Britain.

To do well in the Island, Williams would say, 'depends on accumulation of knowledge, adopting the right approach and consistency of the engine'. He had taken the lap record off Grant the previous year on a 500cc Suzuki and was strongly fancied to take it higher.

Disappointment came as early as Braddan Bridge, where he stopped to find out why the temperature gauge was near boiling point. A mechanic had left a rag over the radiator of his works Suzuki. Both the bike and his temper cooled sufficiently for him to continue but, just when he felt that he was catching leader Grant, disaster struck again at Cregny-Baa when he came off the machine.

Grant, in fact, reckoned that he had matters completely under control, especially as he knew that Phil Read posed the only other threat. Read, making a much-publicised comeback to the Island after boycotting the event on safety grounds, was unable to come to terms with his ill-handling Honda following two superb victories earlier in the week.

Tests in practice showed a recurrance of the chain problem with Grant's Kawasaki, so the plan was to build up a 40-second lead after three laps, when a fuel stop would be made, and then adjust the chain. The chain in fact began to jump on the second lap, but he made it into the Glencrutchery Road pits on schedule and constant practice that week made the refuelling exercise a time and motion expert's delight.

(With the 750 Kawasaki, neat oil went into the big ends via an oil pump, while a 32 to 1 petrol/oil mix went into the fuel tank. But with oil being splashed about by the big ends, the effective burnt oil ratio was around 25 to 1.)

With the tank topped up, mechanic Nigel Everett took 15 seconds to make the necessary adjustment to the 101-link Regina chain to leave the required three-quarters of an inch play.

The chain began to pitch again on the fifth

lap, however, and on the last lap a slight amount of throttle in the first three gears would set the chain bucking.

As I anticipated the Mountain, I was worrying myself sick over whether the chain would snap in the same place as it did in 1975. Had I not handled the throttle with a touch like a midwife's, the chain would certainly have gone.

He went relatively slowly past the Bungalow at the top of the Mountain and caused panic back in the pits when Manx Radio relayed the message that he was looking down at his bike. But with the help of good information from his four official signalling points (Laurel Bank, the Gooseneck, Windy Corner and the pits) Grant knew he had built up a sufficient advantage to slow down on the final lap. Such is the fanatical interest in the Isle of Man that there were also dozens of unofficial signs hung out to show Grant the extent of his lead.

When Grant rode the TT for John Player Norton he was using the same signal-board man as team-mate Peter Williams, stationed between Waterworks and the Gooseneck. Williams took a tight line – almost clipping the wall – so the signaller would stand almost in the middle of the road to indicate his position. Grant's line that year, however, was up the centre of the road and he almost collided with the unsuspecting JPN man, who was totally unprepared for anyone on that line.

Grant's specially-made signalling boards have slots on one side to take the numbers for position and time interval between the men in front and behind. On the other side is a blackboard to indicate any important changes in the race pattern, such as a rival coming rapidly through the field.

I need to have a complete picture of what's going on behind me. The layman just doesn't realise how isolated the rider is out there; if he's first or 21st, he might not know without seeing a signal board.

Whether I act on the information is up to me. If I think I'm going as fast as I can and the gap between me and the guy behind is still closing, then I'd have to think about finishing second. No signal which says 'Go faster' will make me do that. I'll do what I think is possible and no more. Often, my wife Carol tells little fibs when she's signalling but I can usually tell when she's doing it. She might give me information to suggest that the bloke behind is catching me quicker than he actually is, just to try and make me go faster, but I know how her mind works, fortunately.

As he pushed his Kawasaki along pit lane in 1977, submerged under a sea of arms offering him congratulations, Grant felt disappointed when he heard Peter Kneale broadcast over the loudspeakers a speed of 110·76 mph. But he soon discovered the facts: that was his average race speed. His fastest lap was

112·77 mph, which gave him back the absolute lap record – and captured all the headlines.

I never make predictions because you appear such a fool if you're wrong, but I did say someone would have to do a 112 mph lap to win.

The following year he again correctly forecast a 114 mph lap for the winner. Surprisingly, with only two miles an hour variance between each lap, he can tell which are the quicker laps of the six.

My fastest lap was the first, because I really gave it some welly. But it was from a standing start, which cost four or five seconds and the bike had a full tank of fuel, losing a few more seconds. That first lap I was not far off the limit. The second wasn't so far off, either, but I had a flying start and finish, 30 per cent less fuel and I was into the swing of the race, so that had to be the fastest recorded. This is the same every time in a six-lapper. On the third lap, you're slowing down to refuel and, with the fourth, you're beginning again from a standing start and a full tank. On the fifth lap, you should have built up a lead, so you're more interested in protecting the motor, while on the last lap you're cooling down. As soon as I have established a lead, I'll knock it off as much as is necessary in the Island.

Grant had, in fact, recovered from the shock of taking the slip road at Ballacraine on the first lap. At the end of the fast straight, nothing happened when he stood on the back brake pedal and only by constant pumping of the pedal made the hydraulic system effective by Ballaugh Bridge.

Grant's biggest disappointment in TT racing was that his big rivals in the 1978 Classic went out before the race really warmed up. Potentially, it had the makings of one of the finest road circuit races yet seen. Previously unheard of speeds were anticipated from the works Suzuki of John Williams, the semi-works Yamaha of the legendary Mike Hailwood in his comeback year and from the factory Kawasaki ridden by Grant. Also there was Tom Herron on his private Yamaha, who had already tucked away the Senior TT that week.

By Ballacraine, Grant and Hailwood were level on time and many of the 40,000 spectators believed that 'Mike the Bike' would pull off a sensational win to add to his Formula One success at the beginning of the week. Hailwood's Yamaha, however, holed a piston on lap one and he was out. Herron, with his bike spluttering, was passed at Braddan Bridge, while John Williams was taken on the Mountain Mile . . . moments after Grant discovered that Hailwood was out.

The leader on the road, Joey Dunlop, was overtaken past the Bungalow, so Grant headed the field both on the road and on time.

Tom Herron, the Ulsterman, rode road circuits as well as anyone

If any lap was to produce a new record it would be his second and Grant, with clockwork precision, notched up his marvellous 114·33 mph on cue.

I have always followed the old riders' advice that you should win races at the slowest possible speed but I have fallen victim of the press, who deliberately manufacture these artificial speed barriers in the form of TT lap records. There are two things to do in the TT – win at the slowest speed and go quicker on one lap to ensure you top the lap record. So I did just that.

Williams, preferring to ride a 500cc Suzuki because he thought it would be better suited if it rained, was out-gunned and plagued with brake failure; Grant had no difficulty from other riders in collecting his second successive £6,000 and a further new lap record. But it was a nerve-wracking ride for the normally unflappable Grant. On the fourth lap, as he hurtled towards Ballacraine, back brake trouble struck again.

In the fortnight leading up to the race, Grant had had the 750cc Kawasaki engine re-mounted completely, which made the rear

engine mounts much stiffer. As the engine was held more rigidly in the new frame – produced with the help of Ken Sprayson and Ron Williams – there was more vibration than usual and the weak spot was where the brake master cylinder was welded to the chassis. As Grant braked from 160 mph, the master cylinder and its holding bracket fell down by his left foot, leaving him to rely only on the double front discs.

When I spotted it, I knew it could not get into the chain and have me off, so long as I trapped it securely with my boot. It was safe, provided I allowed myself extra room braking into bends.

Grant toyed with the idea of pulling into the pits to have it removed, but he realised that the chances of him being allowed out again by TT officials were slim, to say the least. On the penultimate lap, the rod holding the master cylinder broke and the complete assembly dropped off at Parliament Square in Ramsey. Anguished marshals collected the cast-off part from the road and there was a strong possibility of Grant being black-

Mr. and Mrs. Grant with the TT Classic trophy

As he careered down the Mountain and on his way to Douglas, he began to think of the risk of being excluded from the race because of the missing back brake. He made his decision and the grandstand crowds were staggered to see the green and white machine roar past an equally bemused pit crew.

Out of the corner of my eye, I could see Nigel stood trembling with this big fuel can and his mouth wide open as I went through flat out in fifth gear. It was comical to see the vacant look on his face. After the race, we found there was a litre and a half left in the tank, which was a bit too close for comfort.

I know there was a question of me being black flagged and it had been reported around the circuit that something was dangling down, but I think common sense prevailed. No top rider over there will do anything daft, and that includes me.

Had I been black flagged I think I might even have carried on, knowing it wasn't dangerous, and argued about it afterwards.

It tickled me pink to get safely round at 112 mph without a back brake. It won't be in the record books, but it pleased me to know I could tour round at 112 mph in that state.

Grant and his many followers were again delighted at the success and he once more became the toast of the Island. Kawasaki UK were understandably pleased with both man and machine – they had kept the factory's name in the public eye for four years. Grant, however, was a little upset to hear the team management were unhappy about his modifications to the chassis. They also suggested that Grant's mechanics had forgotten to screw up the brake cylinder, and that this had caused the trouble.

I couldn't see why there had to be any questions asked. We'd done the job which was required, won the big race and set a new lap record as well. How it was achieved should not have mattered as long as it didn't involve cheating.

If anyone has helped Grant become one of the really special TT riders, it must be former Irish champion Billy McCosh, who once lapped the Island on a Matchless G50 at a splendid 98 mph. He knew the classic lines and was able to impart this knowledge to Grant. In the 1973 F750 TT, McCosh watched critically from Rhencullen and could hardly believe that Grant had lapped at 104 mph to come second. Grant, it seemed, was on the wrong side of the road! Thanks to the Irishman's tuition, Grant has since been able to take Rhencullen much more professionally. However, he did well to coax the smoking John Player Norton home at all on that day in 1973, as the crankcase had split.

Just as I passed over the line, I could actually hear the bottom end thumping about the crankcase.

flagged for riding a machine in a dangerous condition.

My heart sank, because I thought John Williams would be able to catch me. I had to assume a speed that would keep me out of danger but still be quick enough to keep a distance between me and John.

Grant had a lead of 75 seconds and he went on to win by 50 seconds, rushing past an astonished pit crew at the start of the last lap when they were expecting him to refuel. But Grant, knowing he would have been prevented from re-entering the race, gambled on having enough fuel to cover the final $37\frac{3}{4}$ miles.

Grant had worked out a pre-arranged system to let his pit crew know he would call in if he himself had decided to take on more Shell. As he passed the Bungalow commentary point, he pointed down at his engine, a fact which Manx Radio's Ian Cannell immediately relayed to excited listeners. But this was a planned exercise to notify the team of an impending pit stop for refuelling.

When he finally won his first TT in 1974 –
the 1,000cc Production race – he felt that it
had been just a matter of time after the previous year's performances.

*One of the things I wanted was to win a TT,
yet – no matter how hard I tried – it never
seemed to go completely right. But the first is
always the hardest, whatever it is you're doing.*

He achieved the breakthrough on Les Wil-
liam's famous 748cc three-cylinder Triumph
Trident, nicknamed 'Slippery Sam' because
of its history of losing more than a few
globules of oil en route! With his right wrist in
plaster after breaking a bone at an earlier
mainland meeting, it proved an uneventful
four-lap ride on the reliable four stroke, apart
from trouble with flies, which always pose a
hazard on the Island during a spell of hot
weather.

Because of the restriction caused by his
plaster cast, Grant was unable to grasp the
throttle with his fingers. With his hand flat on
the grip, he knocked the power on and off as
if he was rolling pastry.

Once, turning round to check the opposition, he lost all three perspex tear-offs from
his helmet and had some difficulty in seeing
thereafter.

Since then, for long races on hot days he
has carried a damp sponge, held inside half a
tennis ball by a piece of knicker elastic and

secured inside the fairing just below the
bubble.

*I rarely use it, but if you do discard all the
tear-offs and a big insect splats like a runny egg
onto your visor, you can slow down and wipe it
clean with the sponge. It's safer to take one
hand off the bars at speed and lose ten seconds
than not be able to see.*

*That Trident never missed a beat throughout
the TT race. It was a beautiful bike to ride and
there's something magical about the sound of a
Triumph three, even if it's a travelling marshal's bike. Whenever I hear the wail of one
being revved it always makes me think of the
Isle of Man.*

Although his 1978 success was the one
which brought him most publicity, Grant
still considers his TT victory on 'Slippery
Sam' gave him the most pleasure.

*There is a very big difference between a pro-
fessional and a personal performance. In terms
of helping my career, the 1978 win was easily
the best thing that happened to me.*

Although he can sometimes recognise faces
on slow corners, Grant rarely waves to the
crowd in the Island until the race is over;
although spectators might feel he is being
aloof, anything can happen before the
chequered flag.

*Sometimes I feel it is my duty to wave to
those who have come to watch me. There is no*

*Racing has come a long
way since Ernie Williams
won the 1921 Junior TT
on his AJS!*

Grant flies over Ballaugh Bridge on 'Slippery Sam' to record his first ever TT win

riders to take up the challenge of racing there.

If there aren't any Mick Grants or Mike Hailwoods coming through, the TT is obviously going to suffer. It may sound improbable, but in 30 years' time we may look back and say: 'Remember that time when they used to race 30 miles round one lap in the Isle of Man?' The TT is so precious to us that we must do all in our endeavour to keep it. We have a history in this country of giving away something that is special and envied by everyone else, whether it be colonies or TT circuits or the British motor-cycle industry.

Provided the TT organisers do their job right, I don't believe there will be a problem getting the riders. Those who don't want to go for whatever reason have a perfect right to stay away. But I believe 99·9 per cent of professional racers who enjoy racing a motorcycle would get immeasurable pleasure from competing in the Island, once they had done their homework.

Quite clearly, the TT organisers should pay good money now to promising young riders to wean them on to the Isle of Man. Then, when they become budding Sheenes, they will insist their factory supplies them with machinery for the Island.

doubt in your mind on a short circuit that the bike is going to last the race and so waving on the victory lap is a good way to relieve tension.

All riders suffer acute embarrassments at some stage and Grant had one of his biggest in the Island.

Everyone seemed to be waving their programmes like mad as I went past and I reckoned I must have gone from 18th to first. What a sight! Really made the blood run faster. I am glad I didn't wave back, because it was Agostini they were cheering on and he was just about to lap me!

Grant – for so long the champion of the TT cause – is less certain about the event in the 1990s, when there may be no experienced

Although Mike's a friend, I believe the ACU did the wrong thing spending a lot of money getting Hailwood back to the TT: it was a very short-term policy. That money should have gone to up-and-coming riders. The TT is so high in popularity now that it will exist in its own right. But, in several years' time, it could start to dwindle when the established runners are too old.

One fan's banner after Grant's epic 114 mph TT lap in 1978

RIVALS

Mike Hailwood

Even if he had not made his amazing return to the TT in 1978, he would still have ranked as my all-time great. He was definitely the finest road racer there has ever been. When he first stamped his name in the record books, there were many others on equal machinery and the competition amongst factory teams was very tough. But to get back on a racing bike after eight years and go round the Isle of Man at 113 mph in practice and then to beat the best short circuit racers as well, that makes him something special. If I came out of retirement after ten years, there would be next to no chance of me being a race winner at top international level. I don't possess that kind of ability. Clearly, Mike's car racing exploits helped keep him fairly sharp, but the guy had such competitive energy that it overcame all the technological development that had taken place since he had been away. It's one hell of a bloke who can adapt to slick tyres and an extra 30 miles an hour as quickly as he did and with such limited practice.

Whatever Hailwood's motives were for making a come-back – and I like to believe it was because he liked riding a bike round the Island – I do feel he cut short his career too soon, before he could give it all he wanted to give.

I recall racing against Hailwood at Silverstone during one of the great man's occasional come-backs. This guy came rushing by like a maniac on a Yamaha and I didn't know who it was at the time. For me, Hailwood was the greatest man ever to sit on a motorbike. With his success rate through the different eras, he has to be Mr. Motorbike.

Phil Read

Phil went on racing for too long. The hardest thing for a professional rider – and that includes me – is knowing when to call a halt. He claimed he was quitting on a number of occasions but did not have the courage of his convictions to keep those promises, which I don't think did him any good at all. But he definitely was one of the all-time greats, as he proved by winning the world 250cc championship on a private bike – that was an incredible feat. His liking for being in the public eye and his love of riding motorcycles made him carry on for so long. He also revelled in the rewards of racing, both financially and from an ego point of view. He was a hard yet fair rider to race against. He always courted controversy and I wonder if he intentionally encouraged it.

Kenny Roberts (left)

He was the most under-rated, if not the best rider in the world before he won the 500cc title in 1978. His personality and sense of humour was stronger than press interviews would have us believe, because he would often come across as a one-word answer man. Although he had good motorcycles, it was the combination of his own natural ability and having Kel Carruthers on hand that made him such a force. To have an ex-world champion as team manager and race mechanic can't be bad. There are an awful lot of people holding similar positions to Kel who haven't a clue what they're talking about. As Roberts proved, you don't need to be a Mr. Universe to ride a 500 or a 750 and, through his American schooling of road racing, motocross and dirt track, he had the experience to deal with any situation that might arise on the track.

Gregg Hansford (below)

Gregg is a sad case, because in spite of so much natural ability – more even than Roberts – he never seemed to have the aptitude for racing. A bit of a waste, really, because if his appetite for the sport matched his talent he would have been unbeatable – another Hailwood. Within three laps, he could break the record on a circuit he had never been to before. His large size definitely went against him on the smaller machines and I felt he rode the 750 Kawasaki too hard. Basically, he seems to be a home-loving person: if the world championships were held in Australia, he would be a clear winner. I know it would be hard for me, as a European, to undertake a full racing season in Australia, but the same must apply to the Americans and Japanese who compete on the Continent. Gregg appears to lack a sense of direction, but anyone can see the value of having a guy like his mechanic, Neville Doyle, by his side.

Steve Baker (above)

The saddest thing to happen to Steve was not being given a second chance to contest the 500cc series with Yamaha. It isn't impossible to win a world title in the first year, as Roberts showed, but it is very difficult. So it was unfair for Yamaha to write him off after finishing second in the championship. His confidence flags at times, but a rider with his ability can bounce back at any time.

Barry Sheene

In all the years I have raced against Barry, I have never seen him do a 'start money special'; considering the number of meetings he has taken part in, that has to say a lot for his character. He has almost an embarrassment of natural ability, but always puts maximum effort into every race. He has the knack of being able to gauge a race very well and will often make a poor start and come through the field from the back. I found it hard to accurately assess how much speed his Suzukis had got, because he did hold power in reserve. Where someone like Wil Hartog was unashamed about letting his bike accelerate fiercely away and showing its full potential, Sheene would always hold something back. Most important of all, he has perhaps been the sport's best ambassador alongside Hailwood.

His tremendous courage is shown by the fact that he was the most difficult rider to pass during his first race after his monumental Daytona crash in 1975. I was last away and he was the final man for me to pass, which I eventually did before he pulled out. My respect for him will always be immense, although he has acted unprofessionally at times by opening his mouth before engaging his brain.

He is the master of the hang-off riding style yet still remains in full control, and his racing lines are so consistently accurate that he could run over a sixpence on a corner every time. The only occasion he is off line is when he wants to be, sometimes displaying a cunning ability to deceive a rider on his tail.

Pat Hennen

Pat had a natural talent to stay on a motorcycle when all others would have fallen off. His style was somewhat unorthodox, even though it was effective – it could not be described as neat. He had an incredible way of learning new corners and often took a variety of lines, but he got his lap speeds right, so who am I to criticise? I was as sorry as anyone when he had his crash at the TT, because he had shown great spirit in going to the Island in the first place. He went as a top factory rider and was not afraid of being beaten.

Wil Hartog

He had been a top rider for so long that it didn't surprise me when he won his first grand prix at Assen in 1977. Without decrying Sheene's performances, when Suzuki farmed out their works bikes, all the riders went exceptionally well on them – none more so than Hartog. It was clear that Sheene cleverly kept secret the machine's advantages, like extra speed. Hartog has the experience to win a world championship. He is level-headed and hardly ever falls off.

Tom Herron

In racing there are winners and there are runners. Without that bit of luck everyone needs, Tom was not a winner. Before getting the Suzuki works contract, he had never won a grand prix event, although the world championships had been his living for four years. His strong personality made him a super chap, one of the real good guys of racing who would always help out anyone. He was a very hard rider, especially when conditions go from dry to damp and, with his extraordinary ability of knowing where the limit is, he rarely crashed. He had the strength to obtain the backing to become Britain's best privateer in the grands prix and that alone was worth a factory ride.

Kork Ballington

From being one of the world's top privateers at the end of 1977, Kork came to grips with the works Kawasakis and went on to win two world championships fairly and squarely. I must admit he was a better rider than I first thought he was. Kork was fortunate to have as his mechanic his brother Derek, whom I regarded as one of the few in grand prix racing who really knew what he was doing. But nothing should detract from Kork's performance: he landed a works contract and took full advantage of it. That's what racing is all about.

Barry Ditchburn (right)

Although we were on friendly terms, we did have occasional difficulties as team mates. He tends to be a little emotional about his racing and sometimes moody, but that's not really a criticism. Riders should be as they want to be. On his day, there was no-one faster, but he lacked a little consistency.

Johnny Cecotto (left)

I never really used to rate him. When he won the 350cc world championship at 19, he failed to be consistent for several seasons after that. When he has his act together, however, he may be the fastest rider in the world and if he could string a few more consistent rides together, he would be right at the top. Unlike most other riders, he often goes quicker in practice than in the race.

THE FUTURE

Excitement is about going forward into the unknown. Breaking a lap record is going into the unknown.

When we had the first television in our street back in the 1950s, apart from the picture looking like a snowstorm, it was fabulous entertainment because we had not seen anything like it before. But should there have been rules and regulations which would have had us sitting here today watching the same television? I much prefer the way progress has brought us colour television and the end of the ten-minute wait for the set to warm up. The same rules apply to motorcycle sport. When the Beo sidecar controversy blew up, there were some ACU big-wigs wanting sidecar wheel steering stopped. It was crazy and downright dangerous to think of curtailing that kind of development. Then there was the call for a ban on slick tyres. If that happened, you'd have to take two sparking plugs off a 750 Yamaha to make it safe to ride.

Close racing between star names, with plenty of 150 mph wheelies, is what the crowds want, according to Grant. If spectators want to witness lap and race records being broken each year, the controlling bodies should make the rules to allow this to happen rather than becoming so frightened that they clamp down on racing speeds.

I very firmly believe machines should be made to fit circuits rather than circuits fitting machines. The administrators reckon the machine has to be made slow enough to tackle a circuit, but this is completely negative thinking. They think the only way to improve racing and to make it safer is to cut down the speed of the machines. I don't think this should be done. It is up to the manufacturers to make the bikes safe at whatever speed they're competitive. People have been saying for years that machines are now getting too fast for places like the Isle of Man; I think that's rubbish.

If I took a machine that did 250 mph to the Isle of Man, it might not be any good to me. But it would be up to me and the manufacturer to sort that one out instead of having people impose regulations. The Japanese can now almost press buttons in their factories to produce whatever horsepower they want in a motorcycle and it has been generally stated that a 150 bhp bike could easily be produced.

This I find exciting because it's natural development. Rather than having a 150 bhp engine which can't be used to its maximum, it invites the experts to work on improved chassis, tyres, aerodynamics and brakes to cope with that level of power. When all those other aspects are up to scratch, the 150 bhp engine will be safe on any circuit that exists today.

Designers of motorcycles are intelligent people and they know they are not going to get first prize for a race just because their machine has 150 bhp and all the others have 120. It's a matter of getting round the circuit with the quickest set of lap times. The horsepower will be no good if it leads to blown tyres or bent chassis.

Any dramatic increase in horsepower at this time would be too much for either the tyres or the frame, or the suspension might not be able to take it and the brakes might then fade. For ten miles an hour extra along the straight, the bike might well be knackered. It's not speed – all the other areas of development have to keep step with increasing power output.

When the lightweight 350 Japanese two strokes entered the sport, only a handful of riders – among them Britain's John Cooper with his Yamsel – could ride them to their limit. They were producing around 55 bhp, but only the talented could master the light machines with their narrow power bands. But within two years, most could ride them quite comfortably. The same happened with the 750 and only a small minority are now unable to race the big machine.

The ideal is to have the weight of the machine as low as possible and the narrowest engine possible. Grant considers a four-cylinder bike would be best designed with its quartet of 'pots' as a double row of twins or with its four in line down the machine, leading to a narrow frontal area, as seen on the Kawasaki GP racers.

The only drawback Grant sees with a four-stroke is the greater cost of producing that type and the difficulty in complying with current noise regulations.

Noise isn't as important as I thought it was. While I wouldn't like racing bikes to be as quiet as road machines, I thought the regulations to reduce the noise limits would kill the sport. I was wrong and the quieter noises are much more sympathetic on spectators' ears.

What really concerns Grant is any possibility of a major move to pull back lap speeds.

That's the retrograde step people just don't

Perhaps the last hope for
a successful British-made
racing motorcycle arrived
with the 750cc four-
cylinder Phoenix, the
brainchild of Barry Hart
(left). Although it failed
to make a significant
impact, there was some
hope for the future – and
Mick Grant lavished high
praise on the bike when
he had a chance to track
test it

opposite
Uncorking the bubbly
after finishing in the first
three at a grand prix are
Kenny Roberts (centre),
Pat Hennen (left) and
Barry Sheene

following page
Acclaimed as the greatest
road racer in history,
Mike Hailwood made a
sensational come-back in
1978, winning events on a
Ducati both in England
and in the Isle of Man

want. There's nothing more depressing than
seeing in a programme that the lap record was
113 mph and the actual speed on a particular
day was 109 mph in perfect weather conditions.
Excitement in life is all about going forwards,
not backwards.

The FIM tried to reduce speed back in the
1960s, when rules were introduced to restrict
numbers of cylinders for each class: 125cc
and 250cc were allowed up to two, 350cc –
three and 500cc – four.

A whole range of brilliant machines became
obsolete overnight, just because some fuddy-
duddies made the decisions. It happened to
sidecars in 1978 and it's sure to happen again.
The FIM are going to keep on chopping until
they kill the sport. Anything new they're
frightened of.

I was sad to see the demise of the 750cc class
because it was a branch of racing I enjoyed.
There was so much pressure put on it by those
who make silly rules and who are not close
enough to know what is happening within the
sport. They argued that 750 bikes were getting
too fast and circuits becoming too dangerous, so
the 750s were chopped. They think a 500cc
machine is safer than a 750, but there's precious
little to choose between them on top speed. They
feel Formula One bikes must be safer than any
other big capacity machines because they look
like production bikes, but it won't be long before

they are as fast as the old 750 Superbikes.

But the 500cc class is definitely the number
one interest for GP spectators these days. I
would have liked to have the F750 bikes carry
on, because they were a break from tradition.
The 500cc grand prix class is so steeped in
tradition that we all used to race for no start
money and, as we all know, grand prix racing
is a very costly business.

When Formula 750 racing began in the
early 1970s, organisers were paying enough
money for competitors to break even on expenses, but it still proved to be a prohibitive
class for hard-up privateers.

Formula One racing has its advantages, in
that spares are readily available at a reasonable price from motorcycle shops, which was
the original attraction of the smaller Yamaha
racers. The basic design of the engine, crankcase and frame of the 250cc and 350cc racers
were exactly the same as those used in the
road-going machines. On more than one
occasion, Grant used a crank from a road
machine in his Yamaha because of the price.
Apart from a few minor differences, they are
taken from the same castings.

It's the brand name that counts rather than
the technical detail of the machine. But it
varies from country to country: in France, the
result of the Bol d'Or might sell a lot of bikes
but it wouldn't do anything for sales in Britain,

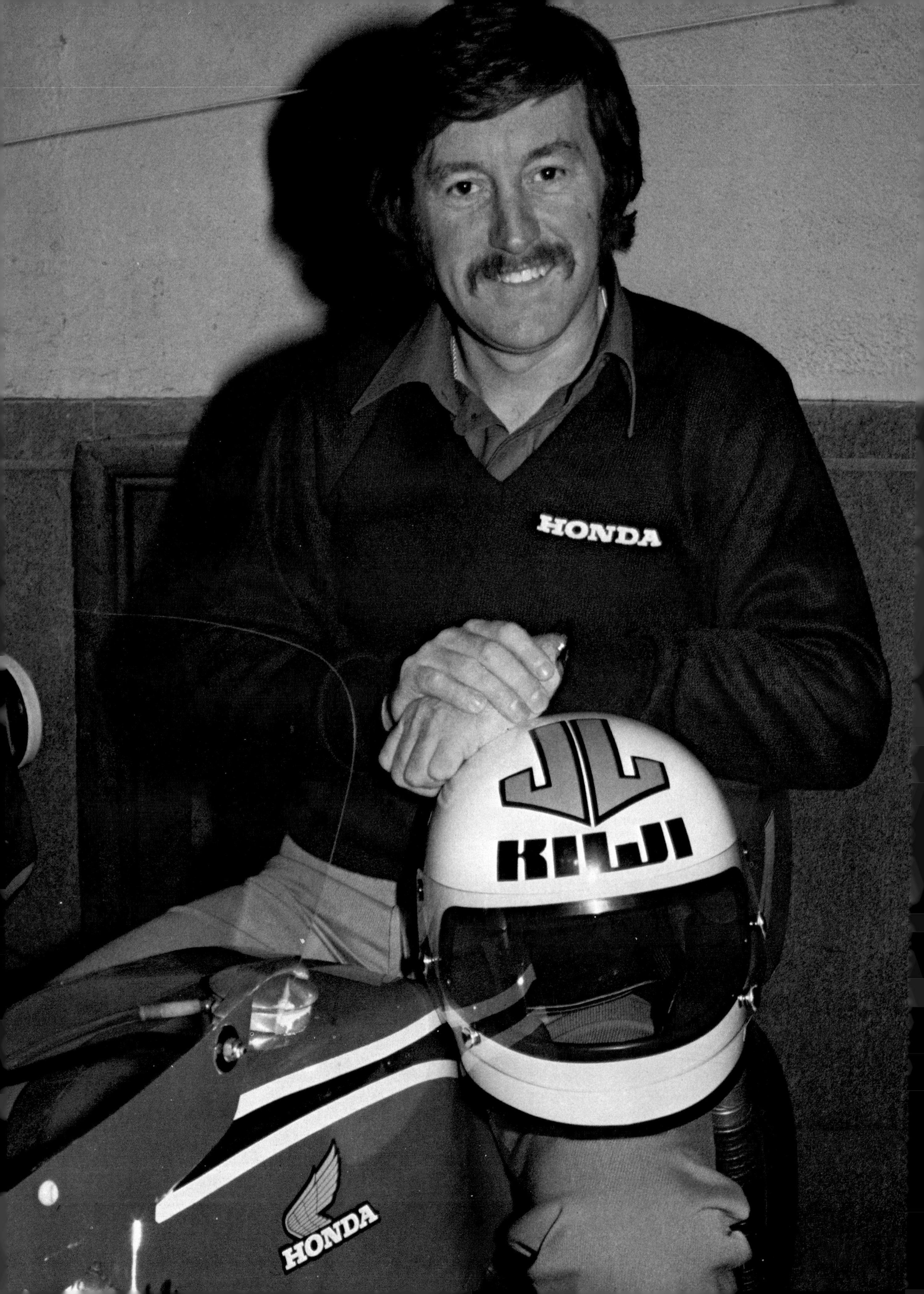
HONDA
KILJI
HONDA

where the TT is the one that counts.

Road racing is almost all about selling the breed these days, not so much about improving it. In the early 1900s, it was all about improving, advertising and selling. The pedals came off for racing, which must have been about improving the breed! These days it's 20 per cent improving the breed and 80 selling it.

Clearly, the pick of recent improvements to road machines has been the introduction of disc brakes and better chassis geometry, both from lessons learned in racing. As Formula One gathers momentum, it is highly likely it will lead to far more improvements to road bikes than the 750s ever did.

Tyre design helps as well. We might be using slicks which can't be used on the road, but the materials used and the constructional know-how will eventually come into road use.

The hope is that Formula One rules will not get out of hand. When Grant contested a Castrol six-hour production race in Australia, he discovered that the organisers were so fanatical about the rules that an exhaust pipe flattened or a foot-rest rubber worn away during practice had to be replaced by new equipment so that the machines were exactly 'as they came out of the factory'.

Prices supported the strong case for Formula One bike racing. While £8,000 would be needed for a competitive new 750cc Yamaha,

around £3,000 is enough for a basic road machine capable of complying with the Formula One regulations – a further £2,000 would make it highly competitive.

A rider would then have a bike as good as anything other than works tackle. As the flow of new 750 racers dries up and bikes are forced to run on old parts and go slower, so the Formula One machine is going to be more competitive, even at club level. The pendulum has now swung away from two-strokes and, at GP level, Honda are proving that a four-stroke has more potential in terms of both horsepower and lightness. Of course, Suzuki and Yamaha may want to carry on with two-stroke racers but, by the end of the 1980s, I don't think there will be a successful two stroke at grand prix level.

Mike Hailwood's 500-4 Honda had a brake horsepower figure of around 100 in 1967 yet Sheene's world championship winning 500-4 Suzuki nine years later was only endowed with about an extra 20 bhp. But Grant insists that Japanese development is only intended to keep them one step ahead of their rivals.

It may be cheaper now to build a four-stroke engine to get the horsepower than to spend millions trying to take two-stroke development that little bit further, because it must be near its optimum development.

But it is in the area of suspension that Grant feels most development will occur in two-

Just about the most extraordinary racing bike ever developed appeared in France in 1977. Called the Elf-X, the bike, with hub-centre steering and a 750cc Yamaha engine, had its fuel tank housed underneath the engine and gearbox. It was designed by Andre de Cortanze, a Renault research technician who was keen to apply Formula One car theories to motorcycles

top
*West German Helmut
Fath worked wonders in
the sidecar development
field, but his flat-four
'Boxer' engine failed to
have the same impact in
a solo, although the 500cc
bike went through a lot of
tests in the hands of
French rider Jean-
Françoise Baldé*

above
*The long, slim 50cc
Kreidler with just a single
cylinder was capable of
100 mph. It even had the
luxury of gas and air rear
suspension.*

wheeled racing. With smaller capacity bikes, very little attention is needed before racing; on the larger machines, with their greater speed and weight, it matters more.

Solos have had telescopic forks since the Second World War and we're still running the things. It's embarrassing, because the telescopic fork must be one of the crudest pieces of engineering ever bolted to a motorcycle – two independent sliding tubes with their strongest brace being the wheel spindle at the far end of the travel. The sophisticated ones have a mud-guard brace to stiffen up the forks in the middle. Even the old trailing or leading link forks had more going for them. I fancy the telescopic forks will disappear over the next few years. Motorbikes of the future will need some system where, under braking or accelerating, both wheels are kept on the ground.

I'm not technically-minded enough to see how to do it but some time ago Kawasaki played

around with an American idea of a bar which looked like a parallelogram. What it did was to keep the chain in constant tension, as with the old solid-rear-end machines, because the rear wheel spindle was in a constant arc to the gear-box sprocket. As well as aiding chain life, the 'foo' bar encouraged the machine to squat under acceleration and it was almost impossible to pull a wheelie.

On braking into corners, it tended to hug the road, but the number of bearings in the swing arm made it impracticable, not because of the extra weight, but because of the many moving parts. Mind you, it wouldn't take a Japanese technician long to simplify it.

Grant has tested bikes with hub-centre steering and feels the device has potential, but like many others who cherish motorcycle sport, he does not want improvements to put the two-wheelers into the same league as car racing.

There's no doubt in my mind that Formula One cars are choking themselves through the way their sport has been organised. The car drivers are so involved in looking after them-selves that they possibly forget the spectators. The Formula One guy rushes from his heli-copter to his caravan, then obscures himself with a helmet, so the public don't have any contact with him. I don't want to see motorcycle racing go like that. The fun in our sport is that it is on a much more personal basis. People can actually see us instead of glimpsing half a crash helmet poking out of a cockpit. And for another couple of quid, the people in our sport can actually talk to the riders. I don't think we'll ever lose our contact with the people, because the motorcyclists I know are, on the whole, much more down-to-earth and level-headed.

Suggestions of a road racing 'circus' of riders, who could dictate with strength to race promoters have never got off the ground mainly because several of the top names earn so much and do not want to risk a drop in their pay. Without the stars, any organised effort to make grands prix pay out more than their normal pittance to the rank-and-file would be seriously undermined.

But an idea to have the world's top 60 riders in their own competition, away from the FIM, is still being mooted. Whether grand prix racing will survive at the current level is a matter for conjecture, but the 'expenses' paid to riders who have failed to collect enough valuable points from the previous season's GP rounds would barely pay for their fares across the English Channel. The reluctance of world championship promoters to pay out realistic amounts is all the more surprising when their attendances can be any-thing up to 200,000 people.

The question is, do we try to break away from the FIM and form our own group under the leadership of a strong man? There should be no problems in organising our own ten-round world championship on a proper commercial level. With men as influential as Kenny Roberts around, there is nothing to stop motorcycling having a body similar to the car world's Constructor's Association. Comparing the amount of money that grands prix make, in relation to what the riders receive, someone has got to do something about the ludicrous situation sooner or later.

Grant also wants to see a change in the British system, which allows riders who are past their best to take part in the same races as far superior professionals.

To promote motorcycle racing to its best, I believe the fastest 30 riders available on that day should be on the grid. By accepting 40 or 45 entries and using a qualifying system to sort out the quickest (after seeding the top runners to the race in case they've a problem in practice), we could eliminate the farce where some riders are lapped two or three times in a race.

As well as deterring these riders from bothering to enter a meeting, a chance will be given to the good, up-and-coming rider who can go quickly and who a club secretary may not have heard of. There can be nothing more frustrating than going to a meeting and being completely out of your class. In whatever walk of life, you are happiest at your own level.

The future of road racing could be helped by improved television coverage and by the introduction of prestige sponsors.

Unfortunately, the people who determine the amount of air time any sport merits are a breed of faceless persons way out of touch with reality. In terms of spectator appeal, we should have relatively as much TV time as sports like cricket, tennis and golf. We just don't get the amount of TV coverage we deserve. Any sport that gets between 30,000 and 50,000 people at a weekend meeting just cannot be rated as a minority sport. Yet the powers-that-be seem to want their own particular sport televised. If there was a system to discover what people actually wanted to see on television, then there would be a lot more road racing put on the box.

Something like cricket is a participant sport, whereas motorcycle racing is a spectator sport. The people watching at a club cricket match are almost certain to have played at some stage in their life but very few of the crowd at the British Grand Prix have actually raced a bike.

Although road racing has enjoyed good attendances at important meetings in the middle and late 1970s, Grant views the long-term prospects as somewhat gloomy. The introduction of more restrictions will, he feels, lead inevitably to the loss of many circuits in years to come.

The road circuits are most at risk, not so much through agitation by 'anti-road circuit' riders, but more fundamentally, through pressure from the public who may feel that their right to have access across such courses is greater than any right of organisers to run a race meeting. Sterner noise regulations and the growing need for building land may also be the downfall of some short circuits, in the long term, at any rate.

In ten years' time, there certainly won't be the opportunity to race on such a wide variety of circuits. As in the past, changes will be radical and far-reaching.

A racing date in the Far East gives fans in Macau a rare chance of meeting a real, live star rider.

INDEX